OVERHEARD IN DUBLIN #LOL

YET MORE WIT AND WISDOM FROM
OVERHEARDINDUBLIN.COM

G000299046

OVERHEARD IN DUBLIN #LOL

YET MORE WIT AND WISDOM FROM
OVERHEARDINDUBLIN.COM

Gill & Macmillan

Gill & Macmillan
Hume Avenue, Park West, Dublin 12
www.gillmacmillanbooks.ie

© Gerard Kelly 2014
978 07171 6435 6

Print origination by Carole Lynch
Illustrations by Derry Dillon
Printed and bound by CPI Group (UK) Ltd,
Croydon, CR0 4YY

This book is typeset in 10pt Garamond Book on 11pt.

The paper used in this book comes from the wood pulp
of managed forests. For every tree felled, at least one
tree is planted, thereby renewing natural resources.

A CIP catalogue record for this book is available
from the British Library.

5 4 3 2

City Tales

A shark's tale

Crossing over the Ha'penny Bridge, a mother says to a crying kid, 'If you don't bleedin' shut up, I'll throw you to the sharks!'

Overheard by Martin

It's all about me

At the Beshoff chipper in Dublin 4. A girl orders two singles. The guy behind the counter asks, 'Do you want them wrapped separate or together?'
The girl replies, 'Eh, would you wrap one of them separate please?'

Overheard by Orla

True

Debate about TV shows on the Luas.

Girl: '*Fair City* is more realistic than *Love/Hate*.'

Lad: 'No it's not! You won't hear "gee bag" being said on *Fair City*!'

Overheard by Anonymous

The dark side

Overheard in Kielys of Donnybrook: 'What do you mean Brian O'Driscoll's a northsider?!'

Overheard by John

Second time around

A D4 girl in a Barnardos charity shop in Dún Laoghaire: 'Erm, I dunno, it's kinda nice but it's, like, almost like it's been worn.'

Overheard by Anonymous

On yer bike!

Overheard at the Rothar Project: 'I wouldn't roide you if you had pedals!'

Overheard by Caitríona

Aber-bum-bie

'I go into Abercrombie & Fitch just to fart.'

Overheard by Anonymous

'Like a Virgin'

'It's been that long since I've done anything it's probably closed up!'

Overheard by Jackie @Jackiem23

Text talk

A girl at Oxegen festival: 'O to the M to the G, I think I lost my iPhone!'

Overheard by Anonymous

Bum note

'She's so far up herself, she could give herself
an enema!'

Overheard by Geraldine @GeraldineOC1

D4 resolutions

In Starbucks Blackrock: '... so my New Year's
resolution is to switch from an Espresso Frappuccino
to a Mocha Frappuccino.'

Overheard by Lorcan

Prickly piles

Two lads are having an argument on O'Connell
Street. One of them then gets on a bus and he shouts
out the window, 'I hope your next shite is a
hedgehog!'

Overheard by Anonymous

The world on your shoulders

Two D4 girls hauling a twenty-four-pack of Bulmers
Light to the checkout in SuperValu Blackrock: 'This
is really, like, so labour-extensive!'

Overheard by Andy

Worst ride of his life

Two lads on a bicycle: the one on the back stretches
his legs out and screams, 'Ah you're wrecking me
f**king giblets!'

Overheard by Stephen @KillerSteveW

Super sense

Overheard on the southbound Dart: 'I got €100 worth of Superdry vouchers for my birthday. That should get me at least two T-shirts.'

Overheard by Yvonne

Caught between a kebab and a hard place

Three a.m. in Temple Bar. A woman says to her friend, 'Come on! We're going for a kebab!' The friend, crouched behind a car, shouts, 'Wait, I'm just pulling my knickers up!'

Overheard by Maeve

Tainted toes

Two girls in Juniors Deli: 'Oh your toes look great! Did you get a pedicure?

'No, I got a manicure, but for my feet, like.'

Overheard by Darragh

Fast food

At 4 a.m., a mess of a girl gets kicked out of Burger King with no pants. My mate shouts, 'Teresa, you forgot your fecking trousers!'

Overheard by John @jq_iladelph

Tap water

A woman in Starbucks on Mespil Road: 'Can I have a "no-ice grande ice water"?' (i.e. tap water!)

Overheard by John

Let them eat cake

Three of south Dublin's finest on Suffolk Street:
'Superdry, the Abercrombie for culchies.'

Overheard by Tara @tdegras

Role model

A child is screaming in town. His mother turns to
him and says, 'Stop that or people will think you
have turrets. Now SHUT UP!'

Overheard by Gavin @gavinrhughes

Willy Wonka

A 'lady' on the no. 65 bus says to her friends, 'All I
want for Valentine's Day is a fella with a chocolate
willy that pisses money.' (What a wonderful image.)

Overheard by Timmy

Hot stuff

A stunning lady jogs past two workmen in the city
centre. One of the men shouts, 'Take it easy luv,
ye'll boil yer waters!' She shouts back, 'Ye needn't
worry, ye'll never scald yer mickey in them!'

Overheard by Anonymous

Cocktail class

At Electric Picnic.

A D4 girl at the bar: 'Two Piña Coladas and one
Margarita.'

Bar staff: 'Where do you think you are, Castlepalooza?'

Overheard by Conor

Gorilla warfare

At Dublin Zoo. A woman walking towards the gorilla exhibit, pushing a pram and with a fag in her mouth, says to her friend, 'Where's this King Kong motherf**ker at?'

Overheard by Anonymous

Careful Mickey!

A father and his daughter discussing a trip to Disneyland: 'I can't wait Da, I'm gonna keep grabbing Mickey!' Dad replies, 'Just like your Ma, so.'

Overheard by Barry @getthemoffye

What a lovely image

Frascati Shopping Centre, Blackrock.

'What are you wearing tonight?'

'Black leather leggings and stuffing my ass cheeks.'

Overheard by Avril @AppleTartFace

Feminists

Girl 1: 'Did ya see Miley Cyrus on the MTV awards last night?'

Girl 2: 'Yeah, it's called being a slut.'

Overheard by Anonymous

Return to sender

A D4 girl in Blackrock: 'What happens to the cannabis that the Gardaí seize? Like, is it brought back to the supplier?'

Overheard by Fran

Yoghurt addict

I was waiting for a friend on O'Connell Street on Arthur's Day and I was approached by a woman absolutely out of her face.

Woman: 'Here love, ye haven got a smoke have ye?'

I gave her one in the hope that she would go away but she approached me again.

Woman: 'Ye wanna buy any heroin 'cause of de night dats in it 'n' all?'

Me: 'Ehh … I'll pass, thanks!'

Woman: 'Je want a few "e"s instead then?'

Me: 'No, I'm grand, thanks!'

Realising she was getting nowhere, she then asked: 'Well dya want a f**king yoghurt then? … de're strawberry – de're masso … ye can just use yer fingers 'cause I'm using the spoon … yer not getting it for free though.'

Overheard by Anonymous

Psychoanalysis

Overheard on the Dart: 'I like to judge people based on what stop they get off at,' says a girl getting off at Sandymount.

Overheard by Karen

Family planning?

In the Coombe Hospital. A patient advises the nurse, 'Only ever have two kids; it ruins the sex. Sex for my fella now is like throwing a sausage up O'Connell Street!'

Overheard by Trevor

First aid

Overheard at an A&E ward at St James's Hospital:

Nurse: 'What happened to you then?'

Patient: 'I was coming out of the pub and someone jumped on me and kicked me in the head. No one gets away with that ... I have people working on it, I'll find out who it was and when I leave here, there will be a dead body comin' in. No one kicks me in the head and gets away with it. I'm gonna sort yer man out ... but can I ask a question?'

Nurse: 'Go ahead.'

Patient: 'How come every time I come in here, yous put a security guard at the end of me bed?'

Overheard by Anonymous

Made in Blackrock

A girl in Blackrock Shopping Centre: 'They say money doesn't buy you happiness but I'd rather cry wearing Abercrombie & Fitch and sitting in a Lexus.'

Overheard by Eoghan

When the dog has better manners than the owner

Overheard at a block of flats on North Strand: a landlord arguing with a tenant; the tenant is holding her Yorkshire terrier. The exchange went as follows:

Landlord: 'Your dog peed in my lift!'

Girl: 'He didn't!'

Landlord: 'He did!'

Girl: 'He didn't, it was me … now feck off!'

Overheard by Richy

Eco-friendly

In Spar in Clondalkin. Two girls are talking about how expensive bin charges are: 'Sure my Ma just flushes most of the rubbish down the toilet, except the bulky stuff.'

Overheard by Zoe

Touchy subject

A Moore Street vegetable stallholder says to a lady, 'Would ya stop touching the carrots! They're not your man's willy, they won't get any bigger!'

Overheard by Anonymous

Freebie

On Amiens Street. A group of girls spot a lad eating an ice-cream with about four large scoops: 'Here, youngfella, give us a lick of your balls!'

Overheard by Steo

Smooth operator

Outside a beauty salon on Parnell Street: a beautician is on a smoke break, when a taxi driver yells over to her, 'Here luv, will ya wax me hairy hole!'

Overheard by Anonymous

Mind the gap

A girl on the Dart says to her friend, 'I don't understand why they have doors on both sides.'

Overheard by Anto

Girls' night out

Outside the Gresham Hotel a woman shouts to her friends, 'Goodbye! I'll see ya later when I'm off me tits!' One of the friends replies, 'Good on ya woman!'

Overheard by Robert

Beemer girl

I was at a petrol station in Dalkey, and there was a young girl, aged about 19 or 20, filling up a brand new BMW X5. She finishes up and goes inside and as she is picking up her bottle of Evian, a guy comes up to her and says, 'Is that your BMW X5 out there? It's blocking my way.' She doesn't even look at him and casually replies, 'Uhmm, I don't think so, I drive a Beemer.'

Overheard by Killian

Tissues and issues

Overheard from a toilet cubicle in McDonald's:
'Jaysus, it's like pulling tissue paper out of a cat's arse!'

Overheard by Anonymous

If you gotta go, you gotta go

On the Luas to Tallaght. It has been stopped at the Four Courts for about ten minutes.

Overheard the following exchange:

Man: 'Jaysus, I'm dying to go for a p*ss!'

Woman: 'Go outside and do it on the back of the tram.'

The man goes outside. About 20 seconds later.

Woman: 'Jaysus, hurry up, the doors are closing!'

The man jumps on while zipping up.

Woman: 'Dah was close!'

Man: 'I know, but it's still trickling down me leg.'

At that moment I remembered why I love this city.

Overheard by Anonymous

Saxon blood

While at a meeting in a Dublin rugby club, one guy turned to the other guy and said, 'Gosh, Collie, you must have Protestant blood in you, you have a hell of a tan at the moment.'

Overheard by Thomas

Dripping the light fandango

Overheard in the ladies bathroom in Buskers Bar:

'Hurry up Jacinta!'

'Will ya wait for f**k's sake, me fandango is still wet!'

Overheard by Aoife

Maid in McDonald's

A D4 guy asks his girlfriend in a crowded McDonald's, 'OMG babes, squeeze this spot for me? It's totes painful.'

Overheard by Ellie @xLadySmythx

Hovering

In The Wright Venue, Swords. A girl hovers over the toilet. Her friend asks, 'Why are ya hoverin'?' The girl replies, 'I can't sit on that, there'll be STIs bleedin' crawlin' down me legs!'

Overheard by Ella

Totes embarrassing

In Kielys of Donnybrook.

Barman: 'What do you want?'

Ross O'Carroll-Kelly wannabe: 'Can you give me a pint of Heino and a G'n'T for the dolly?'

Overheard by Cian

Great investment

Overheard today: 'Yeah, borrowed seven quid off me Ma for the cinema, spent it on six cans of Dutch and got f**ked!' (The future is in good hands!)

Overheard by Sean @Seancarey2013

Future mum of the year

Pregnant woman (with can!): 'Ah Jaysus, it's gonna be fifteen more weeks. Like watchin' a kettle boil.'

Overheard by Ronan @ronanfla83

Tea vs ride

A tired female party-goer on the Nitelink: 'Ah the best thing in life is a cup of tea.' A lad nearby goes, 'You've obviously never had the ride, have ye?'

Overheard by Ryan

Righteous rugby

A D4 guy in Starbucks Blackrock discussing the previous night's movie on RTÉ: 'The worst thing about *What Richard Did* was that he let the St Mary's senior cup team down!'

Overheard by Aindriú @AndrewRCrowley

Allergies

A friend and I were waiting for a bus back to
Ashbourne, when a young lad approached my
friend with a plastic Centra bag full of obviously
stolen Lynx deodorant cans.

Lad: 'Ya wanna buy some Lynx?'

My friend (a little nervous): 'No thanks, I'm allergic
to the spray.'

Lad (quick as a flash): 'Yeah ... are ya allergic to
knuckles?'

Overheard by Anonymous

Stylist

A woman on Abbey Street shouting to another
woman wearing very short shorts: 'Sorry, love,
your arse cheeks are hanging out!'

Overheard by Stuart @StuWilson1702

Helpful

On the Nitelink. Some fella is puking outside. His
girlfriend, who is on the bus, says, 'Come on, you
can get sick on the bus!'

Overheard by Tony @rocknchef

Calorific

In Kielys of Donnybrook. A young rugger hugger
looking for Bulmers Light pushes her way to the
front of the maul and says, 'Borrman, two Diet
Bulmers, please!'

Overheard by Nathan

Consumer Affairs

Four-seat toaster

In Power City.

Sales assistant: 'What make of toaster are you looking for, luv?'

Woman: 'I don't care as long as it's a four-seater; I'm fed up with queuing every morning!'

Overheard by Trish @Trish_Nugent

About as cultured as a yoghurt!

Sales assistant at Abercrombie & Fitch: 'We don't just sell clothes, we sell culture.'

Overheard by Shannon

Fat cat

Two ladies chatting in SuperValu:

Lady 1: 'Did you know Mars make Whiskas?'

Lady 2: 'Really? I guess that explains why my cat is so fat!'

Overheard by Owen

The curtain whisperer

Two men are looking at curtains in IKEA. One of them says, 'I can't decide, those curtains just don't really speak to me.'

Overheard by Terry

A decent pint

At Dundrum Town Centre, a girl is trying on a tube top dress with a cream band around the top. Her boyfriend says, 'A Jesus love, you look like a pint of Guinness in that!'

Overheard by Aidan

The walking barcode

In Dunnes Stores, a man who forgot his clubcard says to the cashier, 'Do you know what, luv, I'm thinking of getting the barcode tattooed on my hand!'

Overheard by Gerry

This is no ordinary supermarket

In Marks & Spencer, Dundrum. A member of staff shouts to a colleague for help. His colleague replies, 'Stop shouting, this isn't Lidl!'

Overheard by Mary

The other half

In NEXT menswear, a man trying on a shoe asks the assistant, 'Do ye have the correspondence to that?'

Overheard by David @davidmcginn_ie

Duh!

In the Nike Factory Store in Blanchardstown.

Girl: 'It's all Nike!'

Overheard by @BarryEoin

Curtains

In Penneys.

Girl: 'Look at dem leggings'

Nan: 'Jaysus, you'd look like you're wearin' a pair of curtains!'

Overheard by Emily @emilyg0rman

Spudnik

On my lunch break, I popped into the local SuperValu to buy a sandwich. I went to the self-service checkout and there was a fella in front of me paying for his items. He was doing a 'weigh and pay' and couldn't find the vegetable in the alphabetical option. An assistant came over and asked, 'Are you okay?' He said, 'Yeah I can't find spuds in the menu.' The woman replies, 'That's because it's under "p" for potatoes!'

Overheard by Deirdre

Put her under pressure

In Penneys.

Woman: 'I'll be in the underwear section.'

Man: 'Jaysus, you only bought knickers last week. I'm still wearing my Italia '90 boxers!'

Overheard by Eddie

Forbidden fruit

In Penneys.

Young girl: 'But Ma, why can't I have them?'

Mother: 'Because until you know why, you'll not wear anything with "Juicy" spread across the arse.'

Overheard by Anonymous

Do the maths

In SuperValu, Blackrock. A woman says to her friend, 'I'm not paying half price for that, I'll wait until it's "buy one get one free".'

Overheard by Mattias

Kids will hang you out to dry

In SuperValu, Knocklyon. As two women say a quick 'hello' to each other, a little girl asks loudly, 'Mammy, is that the lady you don't like?'

Overheard by Anonymous

Calorie counter

In Tesco, a manager says to the cashier, 'You can't comment on customer's items.' The cashier replies, 'I was only telling her how many calories are in those wraps!'

Overheard by Karen

An easy mistake to make

In Tesco, at the frozen dessert section, an elderly mother says to her daughter, 'Where's the Tom and Jerry's?'

Overheard by Simon

Terms and conditions apply

A lady in Brown Thomas in the Nespresso section: 'I bought all these coffees last week, drank them and didn't like them at all. Can I have a refund please?'

Overheard by Alan @alanwalsh83

Da shine

I was shopping in American Apparel when a girl came up to me with a pair of jeans in her hands saying, 'Hey, do you have these in da shine?' I'm guessing she was looking for disco pants.

Overheard by Síofra

GMO chicken?

A lady in Marks & Spencer asks, 'Are the four-pack chicken legs from the same chicken?'

Overheard by John @EnnisJohn

Bra

In Penneys, a woman perusing the bras settles on a black strapless number. Then she phones her friend saying, 'How'rya! You were lookin' for a black bra, right? Okay, I'll get this one for ya as yer pressie, it's only a fiver, like, but I'll just need to borrow it tonight for me dress goin' to the party … alright … great … see ya!'

Overheard by Mart

Bag woman

Lady shopping at Tesco: 'I need bags, the hard ones, you know which ones I mean? The big and hard ones!'

Overheard by Clare @dublinclare

Dimensions

A mother asking her son in the Pavilions Shopping Centre in Swords: 'Which is smaller, small or extra small?'

Overheard by David @DavidBrano

A bargain!

A man in Dunnes Stores meets an old buddy who asks, 'Ah how's it going? What're you doin' here?' To which his buddy says, 'Just got a bag of spuds for me missus.' The man replies, 'That's not a bad swap!'

Overheard by Bengunn

Gillette Hellfire Power Fusion Platinum

An older gentleman in a tweed jacket and cap says to the cashier in EuroSpar, 'Fifteen euro for razor blades? Were they forged in the fires of Hades?'

Overheard by Anonymous

Sign of the times

Two teenagers in HMV Grafton Street.

Boy: 'I don't know how this place works.'

Girl: 'It's like iTunes, but in a building.'

Overheard by Dicey

A well-mannered bedspread

Overheard a woman in House of Fraser, Dundrum, describing a bedspread as being 'very civilised'.

Overheard by Lynne @Lynne90

Does exactly what it says on the thin

Overheard at Aldi, Liffey Valley:

Middle-aged lady 1: 'Look at this! Paint and varnish remover!'

Middle-aged lady 2: 'What does that do?'

Overheard by Loopy Lou

Knitwit

Overheard at Barnardos Charity Shop, Rathmines:

Woman: 'I think it's too big for my head. Is this a child's knitted hat?'

Shop assistant: 'No, it is a tea cosy.'

Needless to say she didn't buy it.

Overheard by Aine

Not a multitasker

Overheard at Bloomfields Shopping Centre, Dún Laoghaire. A couple walk up to a Tesco staff member who is packing the Easter egg section.

Girl: 'Sorry, do you do Black Magic?'

Worker: 'Eh ... no. I only pack shelves.'

Overheard by Anonymous

The Holy Grail

Overheard in Dunnes Stores: 'Just pass through the ladies underwear and you'll find what you're looking for at the other side!'

Overheard by Anonymous

Bag man

Overheard in Eason's: 'Would you be alright for a bag?'

Man: 'Jaysus no, I'd be a terrible bag.'

Overheard by Trevor

Branding brilliance

Overheard in Jervis Centre: 'I love the Ramones brand of clothes. I wish they did other things, not just T-shirts and all.'

Overheard by Bam @BamKatraz

How short is too short?

I picked up a short dress in Dunnes Stores, and a random lady said, 'Jaysus luv, if you buy that dress you'll need to get matching knickers.'

Overheard by Clodagh @dodibee78

Smart ass

A man at the SuperValu cheese counter in Walkinstown: 'Does your food contain horse, luv?'

Deli assistant: 'Definitely not!'

Man: 'What about your mascaPONY cheese then?'

Overheard by Robbie

Too much effort

A Tesco cashier holds up an item to a customer and asks: 'What's dat?'

Customer: 'An avocado.'

Cashier: 'Av-a-wha'?'

Customer: 'Avocado.'

Cashier: 'Ah, f**k it.' (He throws it into the bag without scanning it.)

Overheard by Mairead

Equality campaigner

A woman in Brown Thomas says to her friend, 'Mannequins; it's not politically correct, is it? Surely they should be called peoplequins?'

Overheard by Michaela

Culture Clash

Out of the mouths of babes

After a fortnight of bad weather. While waiting
in Mary Street, I overheard two Germans asking
a young Irish lad, 'Does it rain every day in
Ireland?' He answered, 'How would I know,
I'm only twelve!'

Overheard by Marty

Do your research

'I think it's called hurling', says an American lady
watching the cricket in Trinity.

Overheard by Frank @bonuschief

Mixed messages

An American girl in the Temple Bar pub overhears
something about 'Fergie' retiring: 'Oh no, she's my
favourite Black Eyed Peas member!'

Overheard by Evan

Talk to Joe

A Brazilian guy asks his Irish co-worker, 'Why don't the Irish go to the streets and protest like us?' The Irish guy replies, 'Ah, it's much easier to ring Joe Duffy instead.'

Overheard by Collie

Trackie trends

Two American girls in town for the weekend make a derogatory observation: 'Dubliners have a weird love for tracksuits.'

Overheard by Padraic

Bleedin' massive

In Copper Face Jacks, an Irish girl approaches a French girl, 'You look bleedin' massive in that dress!' The French girl's friend reassures her, 'That's a good thing in Dublin!'

Overheard by Nicole

Cultural cowboys

Two American tourists in a Temple Bar restaurant ask a waiter, 'So, when it says "Champ" on the menu, that's not the dog food, right?'

Overheard by Anonymous

A sausage surprise

Girl at Oktoberfest: 'What type of sausages have ya?'

German vendor: 'Bratwurst, Würstchen or Bierwurst.'

Girl: 'Have ya any Denny, no?'

Blank look from the German.

Overheard by Brian

She's bananas

In a grocery shop in the North Inner City. An Indian man is queuing to pay, carrying a load of fruit in his hands. The elderly woman in front of the queue turns and asks him, 'What's all that for?' The man replies, 'It is for my prayer tomorrow' (for Dasara, a Hindu holiday), to which she replied, 'Ah yeah, Legion of Mary is it?' and cracked up laughing ...

Overheard by Trio

Guinness split

Two Americans in The Foggy Dew pub: 'May we have a pint of your Guinness please? Oh, and can I get you to pour it into two glasses?'

Overheard by @Fairport_Fee

Is féidir linn

Two Americans on the Dart, going through Kilbarrack Station: 'They really don't like our president here!' They found it hilarious.

Overheard by Ray @GloryDays87

Don't worry, it's just an ice-cream, love

A man on his mobile phone: 'A Polish girl in work
made a complaint against me because I asked her
if she ever had a Wibbly Wobbly Wonder!'

Overheard by Eamon

Sense of sport

Two Americans walk into Oliver St John Gogarty's
pub, the Cork vs Clare game is on the big screen.
Looking confused one of them says, 'I think it's
cricket.'

Overheard by Robbie

Lovely girls

Watching the 'Rose of Tralee' for the very first time,
my Brazilian housemate asks me, 'How come they
don't wear bikinis?'

Overheard by Trevor

Seems Irish sarcasm has rubbed off on our Eastern European friends

I was having lunch with workmates in the Bank bar
on Dame Street. Behind us were a group of three
American ladies, two in their twenties, one around
fifty. The waitress went to serve them:

Waitress: 'Would you like to order?'

Americans: 'Not yet. I love your accent, where are
you from?'

Waitress: 'Moldova'

Americans: 'Where in Ireland is that?'

Waitress: 'Sligo'

Overheard by Stephen

Lovely lingo

A group of Americans ask a Dub, 'Where is the
Spire?' The Dub replies, 'Ah you mean "the Stiffy on
the Liffey"?'

Overheard by Philip

One flew over

In the Two Euro shop. A man buying bird seed jokes
with the foreign cashier, 'How long will it take the
birds to grow?' Goes straight over her head.

Overheard by Joseph

Lazy linguist

A Texan asked me what is written above English on
the road signs. 'That would be Irish,' I explained.
'Irish? Ireland has its own language?!'

Overheard by @cxd147

Yes and America owns the moon

An American tourist in Dún Laoghaire asks, 'Does
the Dart go to Wales?'

Overheard by Eddie

Ask a silly question ...

An American tourist in Temple Bar asks a local, 'Do you know which side of the Liffey we are on?' The Dub says, 'Yeah' (and off he walks).

Overheard by Fabio

Holy guacamole!

American couple in Kennedy's: 'My God, why would they serve guacamole with the fish and chips?'

Barman: 'They're mushy peas.'

Overheard by Kennedys Bar @Kennedys32

Breakfast to go

An American in Bewley's tells the waitress, 'My wife wants to go sightseeing but I'd prefer to spend the two weeks sitting here eating black pudding!'

Overheard by Maria

Destination anywhere

An American tourist in Jury's Inn asks the receptionist if trains to London are frequent. The receptionist advises that 'flying would be easier.'

Overheard by Lar

Tardis time

At a guesthouse in Glasnevin. An English tourist asks the receptionist, 'Excuse me how do I get to Nelson's Pillar?' The receptionist answers, 'A time machine.'

Overheard by Glen

Give me an I! Give me an R!

An American at the Ireland v Italy match (obviously his first rugby experience): 'No cheerleaders?'

Overheard by Tony

The Toy Show

A Polish guy asks his Irish workmate, 'Pub?' The Irish guy says, 'Nah, going home to watch The Toy Show.' The Polish guy goes, 'What??' The Irish guy replies, 'You wouldn't understand, it's an Irish thing!'

Overheard by Mick

Last to Know

At the Blur gig in Kilmainham an American tourist was overheard saying, 'These guys are gonna be huge!'

Overheard by Joshua

Breakfast at Bewley's

Bewley's on Grafton Street.

American tourist: 'Tea please.'

Barista: 'English Breakfast tea?'

American tourist: 'I'll just take the tea, no breakfast, thanks.'

Overheard by Sarah

Gerrup outta dat!

In the office today (PricewaterhouseCoopers) a manager jokingly shouts at a Polish worker who is arguing that Polish food is superior to Irish food, 'Gerrup outta dat!'

The Polish man, confused, asks, 'I'm sorry, get up where?' An American sitting nearby, who has been living in Ireland for over 10 years, explains, '"Gerrup outta dat" basically means "please sir, I insist that you cease with talk or actions of the nature with which you have currently preoccupied yourself."'

Overheard by Anonymous

Lovely linguistics

An English tourist on O'Connell Street says in disbelief, 'I can't believe it, they actually do say "FECK" here!'

Overheard by Anonymous

Troll on a train

As the Dublin to Belfast train approaches Newry, a
Brazilian guy turns to his Irish friend and asks, 'Now
are we in England?'

Overheard by Ger

The great divide

A German tourist has a good question for the tour
guide: 'I noticed that the Irish say "Up in Dublin"
and "Down the country". Why is this?'

Overheard by Brenda

Saltwater

In O'Neill's Bar and Restaurant.

American tourist: 'Can I have that coddle dish please,
but could you take out the sausages and bacon?'

Overheard by Saoirse

Bloomers Original Cider

In Peadar Kearney's.

American tourist: 'Can I get one pint of Bloomers
please?'

Overheard by @ohmygentlejesus

Soccer guy

In the Foggy Dew pub, the Barcelona vs AC Milan
game has just gone to full time. An American tourist

explains to a compatriot, '... Barcelona won the series 4–2.'

Overheard by Anto

Ve have vays of making you eat

In Kylemore Café, O'Connell Street. I was having a full Irish when a German sitting next to me asked, 'Vat is dat Black sausage ting on your plate?'

Overheard by James @Carlislef1

Excess baggage

Middle-aged American tourist in Trinity College: 'I feel naked without my fanny pack.'

Overheard by Anonymous

Weather man

On the Dublin to Galway train, two Americans say to an old man sitting nearby, 'Hope we won't need these umbrellas.' The old man replies, 'Sure that's where they make the rain!'

Overheard by Marina @mimmi07

Priority one

Duty-free shop in Dublin Airport. An American says to his friend, 'This isn't an airport, it's a liquor store with an airport attached!'

Overheard by Enda

Single use only

I overheard an American tourist on O'Connell Street say with delight, 'We discovered the wonders of Penneys. It's so cheap you can just wear it and throw it away!'

Overheard by Amanda

TV Licence

Polish girl: 'I paid my TV Licence, so what happens now?'

Irish girl: 'What do you mean?'

Polish girl: 'When do I get the better stations?'

Overheard by Rita

Warmth of spirit

A local greets a tourist at the Tall Ships festival with 'will ya gerrouta da bleedin' way.' Nice to see them embracing our visitors.

Overheard by Anonymous

What are you smoking?

A man smoking outside a pub on Talbot Street gives directions to a confused tourist: 'Do ya see the Spiral?'

Overheard by Fergie @Fergiemcd

Dublin Bus mystery adventure

A couple of American tourists on the no. 41c bus:
'10 pence, 1994. That's still valid right? I guess
we'll see.'

Overheard by Hugh @hughh95

They'll never take our Fig Rolls

The tour guide proclaims, 'Here is the Jacob's
Biscuit factory which was occupied by the rebels
in 1916 …' An English lady turns to her friend and
says, 'Could you imagine, all those biscuits, for free!'

Overheard by Trevor

Somewhere over the rainbow

Two Americans in the Quays pub:

'I thought there would be more of them here.'

'Who?'

'The red-headed people.'

Overheard by Anonymous

TK ignorance

In Dunnes Stores at the soft drinks section, two
Australian guys looking at the sign exclaim loudly,
'Minerals, wha' the f**k are minerals?'

Overheard by Anonymous

From Boom to Bust and Back Again?

Desperate times call for desperate measures

At a Dublin swimming club, where under threes are free. The cashier asks a man with a little girl, 'When is she four?' The man replies, 'When the recession is over!'

Overheard by Andrew @jambbie147

It's so unfair

A girl in Jervis Centre says to her friends, 'I wish I could get me spray tan on me medical card ... costs a bleedin' fortune!'

Overheard by Anonymous

How the other half live

Overheard in Aldi: a D4 girl with her friend says, 'I never realised people actually did their weekly shopping in Aldi.'

Overheard by Anonymous

Brain translate more like

A pro-Arthur's Day caller on *Liveline*: ' ... but Joe those liver specialists would be out of a job if it wasn't for alcoholics.'

Overheard by Fionn

Priorities

An old man in the Stag's Head pub: 'What kind of country do we live in at all? We'd be rioting quicker over Gatland dropping O'Driscoll, than the Anglo tapes fiasco!'

Overheard by Grace

Crouching tiger

A woman on the Dart: 'I think I could fit three houses on that site.' (Are we starting this again!?)

Overheard by lgmuel @igmuel

Old school

A UCD Sociology lecturer tells his students that 'the most shocking thing about the Anglo tapes is the fact that cassette tapes were being used in the DIGITAL age!'

Overheard by Ethan

Fashion faux pas

Overheard a camp sales assistant in Brown Thomas: 'Every time a girl wears a Primark dress with Prada shoes a fashion designer in Milan dies.'

Overheard by Kevin

Toilet humour

Having a pee in the gents in Merrion Shopping Centre. The old guy at the urinal next to me feels the need to break the uncomfortable silence with this priceless phrase: 'Suppose they'll be taxing this next.'

Overheard by Linohead

The good old days

In Stillorgan.

Guy 1: 'What happened to your iPhone?'

Guy 2: 'I walked into a Jacuzzi with it in my pocket.'

Guy 1: 'That's such a Celtic Tiger thing to say.'

Overheard by Aisling

Blame the tiger

At Grand Canal Dock two work colleagues are looking for a place to eat at lunchtime: 'God, I hate the term "artisan". It usually means your food will cost twice as much!'

Overheard by Tara

Pulling together in the recession

On the Luas, a tough-acting guy says to the security guard, 'If it wasn't for troublemakers like me, you wouldn't have a job!'

Overheard by Niamh

No self-esteem required

A girl in Brown Thomas: 'Yeah, like, I know they're expensive shoes but I have expensive feet!'

Overheard by Dee

Little pixie heads

A little boy on the Luas asks, 'Daddy, who's the boss of Ireland? The Tee-shocked or the President?' His father replies, 'The Chancellor son, the Chancellor.'

Overheard by Melissa

Oh, the humanity

'Mammy, I know what the First and the Third World are, but what's the Second World?'

'Families sharing the only toilet in their house, darling!'

Overheard by Shanners @RandomSaint

Drowning their sorrows

I was standing outside the Porterhouse in Temple Bar having a smoke when five very well-dressed posh-sounding English ladies came out of the pub. I overheard one of them saying to her friends, 'You hear so much about this country being bankrupt, but every pub you go into is f**king packed!'

Overheard by Martyn

Irish Miracle

Two men drinking in The Belfry pub, Stoneybatter:

Man 1: 'That Irish Water crowd are an absolute disgrace. They spent fifty million euro on consultancy fees in one year!'

Man 2: 'Ah give them a break, maybe they're installing a system that turns water into wine!'

Overheard by Anonymous

Financial regulators asleep at the wheel?

Three suits, walking out of the Central Bank deep in conversation: 'Do you eat the flake first or do you push it into the cone and save it until the end?'

Overheard by Michelle

Celtic Tiger attraction

Overheard an American at the Guinness Storehouse: 'We just climbed seven empty floors filled by a few posters for the most expensive pint in the world!'

Overheard by Paul

At the oldies protest

Overheard at the oldies protest: 'Ye'd crawl up me hole for tuppence!' shouted through the gates of Leinster House.

Overheard by Barbara @babsbear

Where was he during the Celtic Tiger?

An American teenager in Temple Bar complains to his parents, 'What kind of country has no Dunkin' Donuts?! A stupid country, that's what!'

Overheard by Roisin

Drugs in post-Celtic Tiger Ireland

A woman sitting behind me on the bus on the phone: 'Yeah, he came to their door looking for cocaine, screaming his head off! Yeah ... so they just gave him a bag of washing powder!'

Overheard by Adam

Born in Ireland

Two men discussing the Kerrygold advert, in which a man collects some soil from Ireland to take back to Germany for the birth of his son:

Man 1: 'Does he seriously think he'll get through German customs with a big lump of Irish field?'

Man 2: 'Of course he will ... because of the bailout it's now technically German soil!'

Overheard by Anonymous

Hallmark Holidays

Consolation prize

'I didn't want to get her pearls or diamonds so I got her vouchers for her dry cleaning. It's practical, but not crummy.'

Overheard by Ryan @RJG_C

Christmas politics

'When are we putting up the Christmas declarations?'

Overheard by Fergie @Fergiemcd

Are you sure?

The day after Hallowe'en in Temple Bar. A girl dressed up as Miley Cyrus says, 'I'm pretty sure I snogged a guy dressed up as Jimmy Savile last night.'

Overheard by Lorraine

Ebenezer Scrooge

Two bus drivers chatting at Trinity College bus terminal: 'I just can't do it, Mick.'

Mick: 'Ah it's just two words Tony, "Happy Christmas".'

Tony: 'But I HATE my passengers.'

Overheard by Harry

Irish Mammies!

Mother's Day.

Me: 'Mam, can we take you out for lunch on Mother's Day?'

Mam: 'No, everywhere will be rammed; I'll cook for all of ye.'

Overheard by Marty @MartyMtweets

Thymeless

A lad in Dunnes Stores stacking shelves during the Christmas period says to his workmate, 'We're running out of thyme!' (Probably waited a whole year to say that!)

Overheard by Seamus

What a ride

Broken ticket machine on the no. 15 bus.

Passenger: 'Free ride for Valentine's Day?'

Driver: 'Anytime love!'

Overheard by Suzie @SuzieHeather1

Know your market

A woman in a card shop asks, 'Have you any cards that say 'mam' not 'mum'?' Assistant: 'You're the fifth person in an hour to ask!'

Overheard by @jon_weir

Divine connections

At Midnight Mass in Mount Argus Church on Christmas Eve, a teenage boy says, 'Dad, I can't get a Wi-Fi connection in here?' (Somebody was dragged along!)

Overheard by Rob

Spoiler alert

At rehearsal for the Nativity: 'Eh, why are we rehearsing? We already know the story is the same every year ... '

Overheard by Declan @DecGilmore

Expensive taste

On Hallowe'en night I was the designated trick-or-treater greeter. I opened the door to four skeletons and gave them all sweets. One of them held the chocolate bar in his hand, gave me a disgusted look and said, 'Have you no money, no?'

Overheard by Butterfly

On deer

Christmas Eve in town.

Child: 'Eurgh, my face is wet!'

Mother: 'It's just rain, dear.'

Child, looking at the sky: 'Reindeer?! Are they peeing?'

Overheard by Clara

Henry Street maths

Henry Street at Christmas time, there are loads of stalls selling posters, hats, etc. A woman looking at a Santa hat says, 'How much is dat?' The woman on the stall, cocky as ever, says, 'Two euro or two for five!'

Overheard by JohnD

Big mistake

Valentine's Day on the Luas.

Guy: 'But I told you months ago I wasn't going to do anything for it.'

Overheard by Alex @Alex22cash

What would he use them for?

Walking through Temple Bar on Hallowe'en weekend, my friends and I were approached by a panhandler. We told him we didn't have any change, and he caught sight of the Viking helmet I was wearing as part of my costume. As we walked away he shouted back, 'What are ya going to do with them horns when ye're done with 'em?'

Overheard by Kate

Made in Brown Thomas

Christmas shopping in Brown Thomas: 'Do you have the pearl earrings Kate Middleton was wearing?'

Overheard by Jen @thisisjenc

Ripped

Friends exchanging Christmas presents in Bewley's café: 'I got you a DVD. Just to let you know I already opened it because I burned a copy for myself.'

Overheard by Sinead

North side Santa

From a concerned colleague: 'The Santa in Dundrum Town Centre is more North side than North Pole!'

Overheard by Aisling @ash_irl

Well if it's free ...

Valentine's Day. Two boys on the bus:

Boy 1: 'Are you going to see *The Lego Movie*?'

Boy 2: 'No, are you?'

Boy 1: 'Yeah, it's free if you have a girl with you!'

Overheard by Kim @kim_cromwell

20 Christmas Carrolls

A guy in Spar asks the girl behind the counter for 'twenty Carrolls'. She replied, 'On the first day of Christmas … ' (Nobody likes a smartarse.)

Overheard by Emer

The dog or the boyfriend?

A woman in Eason's is buying a card with the message, 'To my dog on Valentine's Day'. She says, 'Aww, he'll love that!'

Overheard by Barry @getthemoffye

Weight watching

In Dundrum Town Centre, a girl says to her friend, 'So tell me, what did you get for Christmas?' The friend replies, 'Fatter.'

Overheard by Antonia

Made in Dunnes

In Dunnes Stores.

Woman 1: 'Jaysus there's no decent kid's Christmas clothes left.'

Woman 2: 'Unless you have a four-year-old slut at home!'

Overheard by @WackyWitch7

Santa solutions

In Hamleys, Dundrum during the height of the Christmas shopping, a sales assistant asks, 'Can I help you?' A woman with three kids replies, 'Only if you've got a Valium!'

Overheard by Niamh

Sharing the load

In Smyths Toys, a tired-looking woman loaded down with shopping bags says to the cashier, 'It's a bit unfair the way Santa gets all the credit.'

Overheard by Annie

Fact or fiction?

A lady on the no. 122 bus: 'Bless him, didn't Scrooge leave it very late all the same. Trying to get a goose on Christmas morning is terrible planning!'

Overheard by Emma

The oldest costume

A friend answered her door on Hallowe'en night to two 11-year-olds. 'What are ye dressed as?' she asked. 'A prostitute', came the reply.

Overheard by Anonymous

Ad lib

Little girl joining in with Christmas carolers singing 'Silent Night' on Grafton Street: 'Round John virgin's motherless child ... '

Overheard by Joe

Treat or threat?

Mother to son on Grafton Street: 'If you keep it up, Santy won't be comin' down any bleedin' chimbly' (sic).

Overheard by Ciaran @ciaranjay

Holy cow

On the Luas. A man on the phone says, 'Little Eoin is playing an "Alien Cow" in his first Nativity play. I don't know what these teachers do be smoking!'

Overheard by Rob

Holy horror

Overheard at Santa's Grotto. Santa: 'What would you like for Christmas?' The reply from a five-year-old: 'A f**king fire truck.' The mother was mortified.

Overheard by Brenda @BrendaDrumm

Hallowe'en at Trinners

At Trinity College.

Student 1: 'What are you gonna be for Hallowe'en?'

Student 2: 'Pissed!'

Overheard by Lauren

Führer freak

Overheard in Eason's.

'I don't know what to get Nana.'

'Just get her a book about war. She loves anything about war, especially Nazis.'

Overheard by Anonymous

Oh, the irony!

Overheard on Grafton Street: 'Santa doesn't bring presents to little girls who tell lies.'

Overheard by Colm

Namesaker

Overheard on Henry Street:

Woman 1: 'It will be Damien's birthday on Christmas Day.'

Woman 2: 'Really? So why isn't he called … (long pause) … Christopher?'

Overheard by Alanna

Scent of a woman

Shopping in Boots in the fragrance section, a woman says to her friend, 'I could not go out without me squirt.' (Let's hope she meant perfume!)

Overheard by Ali

Dead right

On Valentine's Day in Marks & Spencer, a man is buying two bouquets. The checkout lady quips, 'The big one for the mistress and the small one for the wife?'

Overheard by Greg @odubhuidhe

In the Words of
a Dub

Veggie pushers

Two Mormons are handing out literature on Henry
Street. A woman passing by angrily reacts when one
of them hands a leaflet to her teenage daughter.

Woman: 'Don't be trying to brainwash my child!'

One of the Mormons strongly defends his colleague.

Mormon: 'Sorry Ma'am, but please don't cast
aspersions on my friend.'

Woman: 'I wasn't casting asparagus at anyone!'

Overheard by Declan

Walking dead

'How's Aunt Mary keeping, I heard she wasn't well?'

'Ah she's not too bad; she is just waiting for the
results of her autopsy.'

Overheard by David

Each to their own

'She's into all that new age stuff, things being in their right corners and all; you know that fawn shoe stuff.'

Overheard by @DubsSupporters

Yummy Mummy

On a warm summer evening in Portmarnock, queuing at the ice-cream kiosk on the road. A young Dublin mother with two small kids asks for three ice-creams. The vendor asks, 'Would you like syrup on those?' The mother turns to her kids and asks, 'Would yiz like serum on them?'

Overheard by Emma

Hiberno-English at its finest

'At least de poxy other bus doesn't take for-bleedin'-ever, doesn't it not?'

Overheard by @OGrianain22

A weapon you can eat

Two lads on the no. 25a bus.

Lad 1: 'What vegetable makes you cry?'

Lad 2: 'An onion?'

Lad 1: 'No, a turnip'

Lad 2: 'A turnip?'

Lad 1: 'Did you ever get a smack of a turnip in the head?'

Overheard by David

Bulldozing the Seanad

Two women in the GPO.

Woman 1: 'Did you hear the "no" side won?'

Woman 2: What does that mean, Breda?

Woman 1: 'It means they won't be demolishing the Seanad.'

Overheard by Scott

Culture shock

A Dub in a Spanish restaurant: 'Me gestapo soup is cold!'

Overheard by Mary

No thanks

Amnesty chugger in town: 'Excuse me sir, can you spare a moment?'

Well-dressed businessman type: 'Bite the back of me b*llix!'

Overheard by Robbie

Shoes or Holy War?!

I was working in a shoe shop on Henry Street and a girl came in to bring back a pair of shoes. They were wrecked. There were scuffs on the leather and the soles were completely worn, so I told her we couldn't take them back. She stares at me and shouts, 'Jaysus, I'm just tryin' to bring shoes back, I'm no' tryin' to start bleedin' jihad!'

Overheard by Anonymous

The Lion King

In the Porterhouse, I overheard a young American saying to her friends while looking into her iPhone, 'Oh look, Rihanna has joined the "Stop Kony" campaign, awesome.' A Dublin guy on the next table says, 'Do you hear your wan, it's the biggest interest the yanks have shown in Africa since bleedin' Mufasa died.'

Overheard by Anonymous

The GPO

At Customs House Quay: 'That's the GPO, it stands for "Great Place Altogether".'

Overheard by Jeanna @JeannaGallagher

Wine tasting

At the beginning of a wine tasting event.

Woman: 'Ah here's the sommelier.'

Woman's friend: 'He looks Irish to me!'

Overheard by Anonymous

Dancing birds

Captivated local elderly customer at the Spanish Latin night in the Chancery Inn: 'I love all that flamingo music!'

Overheard by The Chancery Inn @ChanceryInn

End of the line bargains

A girl in front of me in Penneys: 'Oh girls, look, they've terminal leggings!'

Overheard by Leanne @le_matt89

Multilingual

A girl on the no. 39 bus is shouting down her phone, 'Wha'? wha'? Ma, wha' are ye sayin'? I can't understand you, you're talking Jewish!'

Overheard by Karen @K3W

Star Wars visits Henry Street

A group of girls on Henry Street react to a Garda patrolling on a Segway: 'Would ya look at yer man on the hovercraft!'

Overheard by Nicole @Nicole_Lg

Web of deceit

A guy in Fixx Coffeehouse on Dawson Street is talking on his mobile: '... well she's cut off her nose to spider face ... '

Overheard by Steven

Penneys for your thoughts ...

Overheard in Penneys, Henry Street. Two Penneys employees are having a chat.

Girl 1: 'Wha' were ya studying this year?'

Girl 2: 'Sociology.'

Girl 1: 'What's tha'?'

Girl 2: 'It's all about thinkin'.'

Girl 1: 'Like wha'?'

Girl 2: 'D'ya know da way life is all normal ... ?'

Girl 1: 'Yeah'

Girl 2: 'Well sometimes it isn't.'

Overheard by Enda

If you give him ...

A Dub: 'If ye gave yer man an inch he would take a mile. And if ye gave him a mile he would take a kilometre.'

Overheard by Ciaran @LoveCycling

If it wasn't for Cromwell

A lady in Dunnes Stores: 'That flooding in England is terrible, you'd nearly feel sorry for them.'

Overheard by David @gribers

One in ten coconuts can't read this

Mammy 1: 'I'm gonna make some cakes with my son.'

Mammy 2: 'My two love them with icing and a bit of that decimated coconut.'

Overheard by Siobhan @siobhandevoy

Beautifully put

A mother pushing her child in a pram: 'Ya will in your hoop be getting outta that buggy!'

Overheard by Nick @NicksBowel

Hide the rhino

My Da in Dublin Zoo, noticing the presence of an Asian fella: 'Never trust a feckin Chinaman in a zoo.'

Overheard by @matthand21

The wine you like

Off-licence in Finglas. A woman is talking on her mobile: 'Ma!! They have that SHANTY wine, you like!'

Overheard by Anonymous

Lyons or Barry's?

On the no. 17a bus, a girl is describing how good her new fella is: 'He treats me with royaltee!!'

Overheard by Bren @brenfinn_79

What does he do for a crust?

'He's in the army; I think he's a bomb disposable expert.'

Overheard by DJD

As a wise man once said ...

Overheard a taxi driver at the O2: 'I tell ya wha' girls, if *Beyoncé* was playing in me back garden, I would close the bleedin' curtains!'

Overheard by Anonymous

Crunchy

At Dublin Zoo, a woman says to her little boy, 'Jack look at the cheetos!'

Overheard by Eoin

Scrooge?

'He's so f**kin' mean, he wakes up in the middle of the night worryin' that he owes himself money!'

Overheard by @iGarageIreland

A great place for a chat

Two old men are yapping away in Westpark Fitness when a friend comes along: 'Howya lads, looks like you're workin' on your squats ... diddly squats!'

Overheard by Aaron

Bally

A friend of mine recently moved to Bray, after having lived in Bali in Indonesia for a few years. When she was picking her kids up from the local school in Bray, a few of the other mothers came over and asked if she was new in the area. She replied that she was and she had just returned

from living in Bali. To which they replied, '... eh
Ballyfermot or Ballymun?'

Overheard by Jack

Sympathy

'Poor girl. The state of her fella. I wouldn't even get
up on him to get over a wall!'

Overheard by Emily @EmCally

Mutant

Two women in Tesco are talking about their kids.
One complains that her son doesn't listen to her.
She says, 'It's going in one head and out the other!'

Overheard by Ronnie @ronniewalsh

As only a Dub could say

A couple of Dubs at the bar: 'Is it still raining?

'It's startin' to stop.'

Overheard by @sittinondfence

Taking care of the wife

A man queuing for a late snack in Leo Burdock's
excitedly explains to the staff that his pregnant wife
is overdue: 'Ah it's great. We're having her sectioned
tonight.'

Overheard by Hannah

Mythological flood

A woman in the post office is talking about a flood in her house: 'It was terrible! Water was flowing from every Orpheus imaginable!'

Overheard by Tom

A quandary

An elderly lady chatting on the no. 7 bus: 'We don't really know what to do, it's a "catch 20/20" situation.'

Overheard by Cathal

A difficult muscle group to find

A girl at Westpark Fitness in Tallaght says to her friend, 'I'll see ya in the hot tub later, I'm just gonna work on my adbominables.'

Overheard by Sean

Whatever is most comfortable ...

A guy is lying on the ground after being assaulted. His friend who is calling for an ambulance says, 'I have him in the missionary position.'

Overheard by Nick @PhelanNick

When small talk goes wrong

A hairdresser in town making small talk with her customer: 'So what do you work at?'

Customer: 'I work as a trainee solicitor.'

Hairdresser: 'And your husband, is he into soliciting too?'

Overheard by Anonymous

V for Viennetta

I heard somebody accuse a guy once of carrying out a 'Viennetta' against him.

Overheard by Nick @PhelanNick

Fake

My boyfriend's mum on the new five euro note: 'The man in the shop gave me feckin Monopoly money!'

Overheard by Louise @LousHannigan

Lucky her

Newsagent's in Dublin 1.

Shopkeeper: 'How's your wife? Did they take her in to have the baby yet?'

Shopper: 'Yeah, they took her in this morning to be seduced.'

Overheard by Adam

Escalated quickly

'I must consult my banister before going to court.'

Overheard by Nick @PhelanNick

A slight misunderstanding

I was in my local newsagent's on Errigal Road and the owner and I were chatting about cars. We were debating the correct pronunciation of the Audi model. He shouted over to his shop assistant, 'Hey Mary, do you pronounce it awdi or oudi?' To which she replied, 'Oh God I don't know, but I know the other one is definitely called Lidl!'

Overheard by Ray

Now there's a mental image

On O'Connell Street.

'What's wrong with you today? You've a head like a burst couch.'

Overheard by Damo

Colours of a Dublin rainbow

Overheard on the Quays: 'Look at the colours in that rainbow! There's orange and yellow and gangrene.'

Overheard by Síle @GarraiSíle

Marathon man

While in Lidl on Cork Street, I overheard a woman say to her young son at the checkout, 'Ah feck, I'm after forgettin' me purse … here, Robbie, will ya leg it home and get it for us … and don't be long, run like a Kenyan!'

Overheard by Jack

It's All Academic

Well, they're both correct

Two girls are walking through Trinity College, one points to the 1937 Reading Room: 'Michael Collins was shot in there.'

Other girl: 'I thought he was shot in Cork?'

Overheard by Siobhan

Away with the fairies

Two Junior Certificate students discuss *Romeo and Juliet*.

'Doesn't Romeo say "Juliet, Juliet, let down your hair"?'

'That was Goldilocks, ya dope!'

(It's Rapunzel!)

Overheard by Leanne

Learning curve

Two students in Trinity College.

Student 1: 'Are you voting in the Seanad Referendum?'

Student 2: 'Oh yeah.'

Student 1: 'What are you voting?'

Student 2: 'Probably Labour.'

Student 1: 'You haven't a clue what the voting's about do you?'

Student 2: 'Er, no.'

Overheard by Tadhg

The strongest survive

Two Trinity boys discussing why a girl decided to go for a rugby jock rather than one of them:

'Gotta be genetic diversity, man.'

Overheard by Vinnie @cage_playa

Through the gap

A group of students in The Pavilion Bar, Trinity College, come to the conclusion that '1-inch line spacing is the norm; however 1.25 inches should be used only when desperate.'

(Getting through college.)

Overheard by Anonymous

Domestic engineer

A teacher asks her sixth class boys what they would like to be when they are older: 'Miss, I wanna be a stay-at-home mother, they do nothing!'

Overheard by Wayne

Unrequited Love

At Trinity College.

Guy: 'Oh hi, Brittany!!'

Girl: 'My name is Melissa!' (She walks away immediately.)

The guy stabs himself in the chest with an imaginary knife.

Overheard by Fred

Shrove Saturday

At Trinity College, two law students are chatting.

'Is pancake Tuesday on a Saturday this year?'

'Er, I think so.'

(The future is in safe hands!)

Overheard by Anonymous

Optimism

Coming out of the UCD exam centre, a guy on the phone says, 'Well I definitely got attempt marks anyway.'

Overheard by Rachel @ronronzo

Spell it out

DIT, Aungier Street.

Two girls discussing their friend's ineptitude at using computers: 'I mean she's like completely computer un-literate!'

Overheard by Aine

Top Marx

A film student in Ballyfermot College: 'It's a bit of a coincidence though that his name is "Harpo" and he plays the harp! I mean that's mad!'

Overheard by Sean

Fungi drawing

A girl in the DCU canteen: 'Chocolate is the best way to get those "endolphins" swimming around in your brain.'

Overheard by Aaron

Diversity

Two girls in UCD.

Girl 1: 'I'm going to see Noam Chomsky tonight.'

Girl 2: 'Oh, the guy who came second in *American Pop Idol*!'

Overheard by Danielle

Snow joke

A girl in The Clubhouse Bar, UCD: 'Have you noticed that most of the sports in the Winter Olympics are either played on snow or ice?'

Overheard by Gary

Burning ambition

'I have to do fourth year, 'cause I'd only be turning seventeen leaving school and I wouldn't be able to get the dole for another year.'

Overheard by Debbie @Debathy

Out of character

A girl in UCD: 'I'm gonna be excessively slutty for Hallowe'en.'

Overheard by Anonymous

To die for

A girl walking through Trinity College says, '… dying is the number one cause of death in the world …' (Let's hope she's not a medical student!)

Overheard by Peter

Abreast of the situation

In a lecture in UCD last week, the lecturer asks, 'What is the fattiest organ in the body?' A girl behind me goes, 'Definitely boobs.'

Overheard by Rachel @ronronzo

Not for everyone

In the DCU canteen a girl says to her friends, 'I hate when people say, "He's nice once you get to know him." They might as well say, "He's an arsehole but you'll get used to it."'

Overheard by Gary

Motivation

In the DCU Gym, a young lad struggling on his last rep of a bench press screams at the top of his lungs, 'FOR GLENDAAAAAAAA!!!!!!!'

Overheard by Peadar

Ooops

In UCD.

'60 questions in 30 minutes? That's two minutes per question!'

'Eh no, it's 30 seconds per question.'

'Oh f**k, I failed it already …'

Overheard by Aine

A clean break

In UCD, two lads discuss the downside of living away from home: 'I bought shampoo for the first time ever! It's so confusing, too many options!'

Overheard by Philly

People of the year

In UCD, a girl says to her fellow students, 'It was so exciting seeing who the new Pope would be. Just like when there's a new James Bond or Doctor Who!'

Overheard by Anonymous

Legally speaking

Overheard two students in Trinity College:

Student 1: '... but she's your cousin!'

Student 2: 'She's my second cousin and second cousins are legal.'

Overheard by Anonymous

That is the question

Overheard a Junior Certificate student after her English exam: 'They asked about a Shakespearean play, we never did one! We only did *The Merchant of Venice*.'

Overheard by @Triona95

Blighty

Overheard at Trinity College. A girl after cycling over a potato and falling off her bicycle shouts, 'Feck sake Ireland!'

Overheard by Roger

Rivalry

Overheard at Trinity College gate: 'I can smell UCD off you.'

Overheard by @Blouts

Awesome

Overheard in UCD: 'He went on a J1 to New York for three months … and now everything is "dude this" and "dude that"! ... He's from Finglas!'

Overheard by Fergal

Consideration

A student in class: 'Sir, can you be nice about me at the parent–teacher meetings? My Mam's pregnant and the stress an' all.'

Overheard by Anonymous

Bummed

A student in UCD: 'There's nothing worse than that panic stricken feeling you get when you've just blocked the toilet in a friend's house.'

Overheard by Shane

Ode to Breaking Bad

A student at the Young Scientist Exhibition shouts out, 'Yeah! Science, bitch!'

Overheard by Richard

Half your cake and eat it

The teacher asks a pupil, 'Which is more, $\frac{1}{2}$ a cake or $\frac{5}{8}$ of a cake?' The pupil, who has obviously not been paying attention, replies, 'Yes please!'

Overheard by @Fairport_Fee

MILF

The teacher in Science class says, 'The sun is the hottest thing in the universe.' A student pipes up, 'Sir, you've obviously never seen Anto's Ma!'

Overheard by Eoin

Kneady

A student in Irish class says, 'Miss, why did she make bread in the middle of the poem? I don't get it.'

Overheard by Anonymous

Only in Dublin

Ride thru

Overheard at the McDonald's drive-thru on Naas road.

The cashier shouts to his manager: 'Are we allowed to serve customers on horses?'

Overheard by Caroline

Dressed for the occasion

Two pyjama-wearing girls are having a very open conversation in Spar in Dolpin's Barn:

'... and are ya sexually active?'

'Sharen, I'm not even physically active!'

Overheard by Maria

Lucky Justin

A thirty-year-old drunk woman at the Justin Timberlake gig last night shouts, 'Justin, ya little ride bag, ya!'

Overheard by Sophia @IrishHeartbeats

Common courtesy

A Chinese lad tries to get the bus to stop by waving at the bus driver; cool as you like the driver waves back and drives on.

Overheard by Kevin @doyles_day_off

At the ATM

A man queuing behind a guy trying various PINs and services at an ATM in Mulhuddart turns to me and says, 'Is he playing bleedin' Pac-Man?'

Overheard by Vinnie @cage_playa

Summer lovin'

A true Dub shouts at a group of scantily clad girls on Grafton Street in today's sunshine, 'Where are all you women when it's bleedin' rainin'?!'

Overheard by Sean

Made in America

At Dublin Airport as passengers disembark from an American Airlines plane, the air steward says, 'Have an A1 day!' A Dub tells him, 'You're not in America now, buddy.'

Overheard by Adam

Appearances can be deceiving

At Dublin Airport Passport Control, a woman directing people between 'EU' and 'Non-EU' lines approaches a red-haired man with a massive beer belly wearing a full Dublin GAA tracksuit.

DAA lady: 'Do you have a EU passport'?

Red-haired man, sarcastically: 'No luv, Chinese!'

Overheard by Anonymous

Couldn't tell his arse from his face

At Dublin Zoo, in the chimpanzee enclosure, a man showing his kids the chimps: 'Ah Jaysus, sorry kids, I thought that was his face, it's his arse!'

Overheard by Fuzzy

Quality control

At the Ireland vs Serbia game at Lansdowne Road. A dad is trying to buy a horn for his son outside the stadium.

'How much?'

'Three euro.'

'Okay.'

'Hold on and I'll give you one that hasn't been blown.'

Overheard by Neil @noriordan

Charm tactics

At the Jay-Z concert, the rapper finishes his two-hour set and leaves the stage. A girl behind me shouts, 'Get back on stage, ya bleeding bollox ya!'

Overheard by Robert @RobbieLeavy

After you ...

I was walking down to the docklands through the IFSC and there was a taxi parked on the street, waiting on a fare. The Luas docklands extension was only open a few days, and a Luas came around the corner, heading to The Point. The Luas had to stop, because the taxi was blocking the road. Bold as brass (and with a straight face), the taxi driver calmly got out of the car (the Luas driver was blowing the horn now), and said to the driver ... wait for it ... 'Do you want to get by?'

Overheard by Ger

Shrewd operator

Bus tour driver: 'If you enjoyed my driving, my name's Mike; if you're going to complain, my name's Joe.'

Overheard by Samuel @belungerer

B, B, B, Batter me penguin

Chipper in Dublin 1.

Customer: 'Do you do battered Penguin bars?'

Man behind counter: 'No, only Mars bars.'

Customer: 'If I got a packet of Penguins in the Centra would you batter them for us?'

Man: 'Sure!'

Overheard by Damien

Couldn't walk away from this

Walking down Grafton Street with a bunch of friends, we see a guy playing the guitar. We listen for a minute and as he finishes the song, we start to walk away, as he isn't very good. He cries out, 'Ah here! Ninjas killed me family; I need money for kung fu lessons!' We had to give him money after that!

Overheard by Ciwi

Comedian Luas driver

The driver announces on the Luas at Ranelagh, 'Two ticket inspectors will get on at the next stop.' Half the carriage empties. Driver comes on again, laughing, 'Relax, I'm only joking!'

Overheard by Ruari

De Herald

The driver on the no. 15b bus decides to turn off the engine and walk off into a shop to buy a copy of the *Herald*.

Overheard by Annie @DoyleAnnie

Planning a party?

During the Dublin Bus strike at Vue Cinema, a bus driver (presumably) on his mobile phone says, 'I thought the strike would go on until Friday. Feck it anyway, I better cancel that bouncy castle.'

Overheard by Frank

Back in five!

In Keelings bar in Donabate, the DJ says, 'I'm just going for a cup of tea and a ham sandwich, be back in five!'

Overheard by Adam @Darby817

States

In Temple Bar.

A lad goes up to some girls and asks, 'Alrigh' girls, where are you from?' The girls reply, 'From the US.' 'I've never been to America', the lad says, elbowing his mate, 'but I've been in some states, wha'?'

Overheard by Anonymous

Love the bluntness of Dubliners

'Do you have a lighter you don't need? Need to burn a bit of gear.'

Overheard by Michael @MDoyler

A world apart

A man on O'Connell Street, speaking very loudly in a strong Dub accent on his phone: 'Where are ya?!'

Pause. 'What are ya doing in Singapore?' Pause.
'Oh, Inchicore!'

Overheard by Kev

The stork

A friend was in the Rotunda Hospital recently for the
delivery of her first baby. She was visited by countless
medics, each checking out her blood pressure, the
foetal heartbeat, etc., etc. When the umpteenth bloke
came into her room, she simply pulled down the
blanket and hitched up her nightie in anticipation of
yet more groping, to which the bloke explained, 'Ah,
yer alright missus! I'm only here to tune the telly!'

Overheard by Jo

Miracle man

A man running down Henry Street, holding a pair of
crutches over his head: 'They cured me so they did!
The Leprechauns cured me!'

Overheard by Liam

Powers of observation

As Obama is making his speech at College Green, a
young lad says to his mates, 'Jaysus lads, he's blacker
than I thought.'

Overheard by Mark

Spuds

An older man is in a Jacuzzi with some yummy
mummies at a local leisure centre. He says, 'Jaysis
girls, we're like a pot of spuds boiling!'

Overheard by Nick @PhelanNick

He's not wrong

A guy at a stall on Henry Street: '... giant Toblerones, get your giant Toblerones; they go lovely with a cuppa tea!'

Overheard by Tony

Strategic planning

On St Patrick's Day, a senior Garda says into his radio in Temple Bar, 'I think we can upgrade the security status to MENTAL.'

Overheard by Daniel

Got a smoke?

On the no. 39a bus.

'Anto have ye got a smoke?'

'Nah pal, haven't got a bud on me.'

Anto had a cigarette behind each ear.

Overheard by Big Jim @ThatBradyDude

Who pushed her?

On the day of the All Ireland Final.

A lad on the train on his phone: 'Shh! John's wife broke her leg last night.'

Random lad: 'Can I have her ticket?'

Overheard by Eoin @11shifts11

Haute cuisine

On the Liffey boardwalk, I overheard a 'spaced out'
man recommending the following to his friend:
'You get two slices of bread, load it with butter and
pop in two digestive biscuits! Savage!'

Overheard by Vincent

No messing now

Queuing on Dame Street to go to Obama's speech.

Garda on loudspeaker: 'No alcohol allowed!'

Crowd of 3,000+ people, sarcastically:
'Noooooooooooo!'

Garda on loudspeaker: 'Lads, this is serious!'

Overheard by Anonymous

The coke side of life

Overheard a woman in Spar on Talbot Street: 'I gave
up Diet Coke for Lent, so I'm getting a Coke Zero
instead.'

Overheard by Kev

Not a problem for an Irish Mammy

In the delivery ward in the Rotunda Hospital: 'Jaysus,
he's a face only a mother could love!'

Overheard by Paul @PaulMcQuillan76

When all else fails

A security guard is chasing some young fellas
through Omni Park Shopping Centre. He is about
to grab one of them when the young fella roars,
'Ah no, please Mister … I love ye!'

Overheard by Philip

Drinker's democracy

While voting at 9 p.m. in the Seanad Referendum,
I overheard the following: 'I only vote this late, so I
can go to the pub on the way home!'

Overheard by @aoife_mags

Holy smoker

On the no. 39a bus. A stoned guy, rolling a joint, says
to a group of girls, 'Ah howya girls, are ya gonna join
me for a bit of "hash Wednesday" wha'?'

Overheard by Frank

The apologetic cyclist

I was waiting on a bus and when one finally came
along there was a cyclist just in front of it. I stuck my
hand out to hail the bus and just as it pulled up, the
cyclist went past and shouted at me, 'Sorry love, I
only have the one seat!' I was laughing all the way
into town.

Overheard by Ell

Hash brown

A man, as high as a kite, gets on the no. 56a bus and says to a bunch of young girls, 'Never a frown with golden brown, isn't that right, girls!'

Overheard by Pete

Ball games

At St Mark's GAA Club: 'This is a GAA club, turn off that f**king rugby!'

'Yea, stick on the tennis!'

Overheard by Dave @sittinondfence

On the same wavelength

Strolling through Blanchardstown and two randomers shout over at each other:

'Up the Dubs!'

'Weheeeeyyy! … Any yokes?'

Overheard by Graham @Gralala

P.G. Parental Guidance

Lapland

'Da, if I get ten honours in my Junior Certificate, can I get a laptop?'

'Son, if you get ten honours, I'll get you a lap dance!'

Overheard by Ann Marie @PartAnnMarie

Reverse psychology parenting

A Dublin fan outside Croke Park needs to use the toilet so he tells his three young kids to 'spread out in a bunch, I'll be back in a sec!'

Overheard by Anonymous

Generation gap

A kid in Dublin Airport says to his mother, 'Mammy, how old are you?' The mother replies, 'Old enough to be your mother.'

Overheard by Alexia @alexia

Sole mate Mammy

A little boy says to his mother, 'Mammy there's something in my shoe.' The mother says, 'Yeah, yer foot.'

Overheard by Ashling @ashlingon

Good answer!

At Dublin Zoo.

Boy: 'Dad, who'd win in a fight between a sea lion and a lion?'

Dad: 'That depends on the location, son.'

Overheard by Jarlath

Crisp criminal

At Tayto Park, a mother says to her child, 'I swear, I'm so angry with you, I'm likely to land up as a special on *Prime Time*!'

Overheard by Phil @PhilDonohue1

School of life

At the start of the school term, a little boy says to his mother, 'I thought school was just for a week!' His mother laughs, 'Not at all! Sure you'll be doing this for fourteen years!'

Overheard by Anna

Contagious comedy

At Trinity College Open Day.

Daughter: 'Da, I just went to the disease control lecture.'

Father: 'I hope you didn't catch anything!'

Overheard by @OscarOfIreland

Trouble toddlers

Dad, chasing after his crazy toddler in a café off Grafton Street: 'He's just not cut out for civilisation!'

Overheard by Niamh @NiamhDonn

Terms and conditions apply

At Dundrum Town Centre. A mother says to her teenage son, 'You know the deal, Sean, you don't get today's Wi-Fi password until you walk the dog!'

Overheard by Judith

Broccoli

Overheard in SuperValu, Sutton. A mother is giving out to her misbehaving child: 'Be good or I'll buy extra Broccoli.'

Overheard by BarryK

The f**king donkey!

In Dublin Zoo, an exasperated mother says to a whining kid, 'Stop crying and look at the f**king donkey!' (It was a llama.)

Overheard by Kev

A poor imitation

In PC World a boy asks his dad, 'Da, wha will I be getting for me birthday next week?' The dad replies, 'You see that iPad? ... A woolly hat of the same colour.'

Overheard by Dave

Answer to everything

Was on the no. 83 bus out to Kimmage the other day and there was a woman with her daughter (about six years old) across from me. The girl was quick off the mark with everything and was giving her opinion on everything and everyone on the bus. After one particular conversation where the girl responded instantly to everything, the mother turns to her and says, 'D'ya know what I should have called you? Google!' The girl asks, 'Why?' The mother replies, 'Because you've an answer for everything!'

Overheard by Claireyhead

Psychopathic parenting

Three kids are arguing loudly on the Luas over who can sit where. This went on for a while until their Dad lost his patience and said, 'Did you know that in the animal kingdom, they solve family problems by eating their young?'

Confused looks and silence from the kids.

Overheard by Amanda

You can't escape the biology

In Tesco.

A mother says to her little girl, 'I'm not made of money, Hannah! Stop annoying me!'

Hannah: 'What are you made of, Ma?'

Mother: 'I dunno, blood and guts?'

Overheard by Anthony

Myths and madness

A little boy on the Luas asks his dad, 'Da, who'd win in a fight between a Leprechaun and a Unicorn?' The dad replies, 'A Unicorn of course. Leprechauns aren't real, ya thick!'

Overheard by Ger

Need to pee

I walking through Henry Street when I heard a little lad walking with his dad: 'Dad, Dad, I need to have a wee Dad! Dad, I need to pee! I'm bursting Dad! I need to go Dad, Dad really Dad, I need to go! Come on Dad please!' This went on for a little while until his dad shouted, 'Ahhhhhhhhhhhhh find a f**king dry wheel then, you fecking nuisance!'

Overheard by shoey

If only that was true!

A little boy asks his dad on O'Connell Street, 'Da how do they clean the Spire?' The dad replies, 'They use a massive robot called Spiretron, he only works at night.'

Overheard by Colin

Unhappy meal

Overheard at College Green.

Child: 'Da, I want to go to McDonald's! Now!'

Father: 'No.'

Child: 'Now! I want McDonald's!'

Father: 'I'll take ya to SMACKdonald's if ya don't shut up!'

Child cries. Now *that's* parenting.

Overheard by Ciaran D

Father-son banter

Son (about fourteen): 'Jaysus, Da, I wouldn't put me ex out in that!'

Father: 'Ex? The only ex you have is an Xbox!'

Overheard by Will @Will__Metcalfe

Some things never change

A woman complains about her son: 'At age 6, when I told him to go to bed he said "nooo" and now, at age 16, I tell him to get up he says "nooo"!'

Overheard by Alison

The apprentice

A little girl in Tesco is singing, 'Hot Cross Buns! Hot Cross Buns! One a penny, two a penny …' Her Dad interrupts, 'No dear, that would be a terrible pricing strategy.'

Overheard by Maggie

Gender antics

A man shouts at his daughter, 'Amy! Get down! Girls don't climb trees!'

Overheard by Joanna @butcherjo

Looks lotto

A mother says to her child in a shop, 'At least you don't have a fat head like your father's!'

Overheard by Laura @bioniclaura

When you can't find the answer ...

On the no. 39 bus a boy asks his dad, 'Da, how come the sky is blue?' His dad answers, 'Er ... Google it!'

Overheard by Kayleigh

Action!

Overheard at Heuston Station:

Child: 'Dad, why are we running? We've got loads of time!'

Dad: 'Because it makes it more dramatic!'

Overheard by Anonymous

The terrible truth

Overheard in Tesco:

Little girl: 'What's that, Daddy?'

Daddy: 'That's ham. That's Peppa Pig.'

Overheard by Alex @HydrangeaGirl

Stresslife

Overheard at the end of the Westlife 'farewell' tour. A teenage daughter decked out in Westlife merchandise says, 'I can't believe it's the end of Westlife forever Dad!' Her dad replies, 'Don't worry love, I've a strong feeling I'll be spending another two hundred euro at their "reunion" tour next year.'

Overheard by Jen

Up in the world

On an Etihad flight to Dubai, a mother says to her complaining child, 'Why don't you talk to the flight attendant, maybe she can upgrade you to a better family!'

Overheard by Jessica

Django President

A teenage boy asks his dad, 'Who's Martin Luther King?' The dad replies, 'Er, he was the American president who freed the slaves!'

Overheard by Johnny

Parenting 101

A dad says to his six-year-old son on the no. 18 bus, 'Don't be fighting near me, go over there if you want to fight.'

Overheard by Anto @AntoFox1

Planes, Trains and Automobiles

Cutting corners

While on the no. 37 bus into town, the bus driver announced, 'This bus is behind schedule so I'm turning it into a no. 39.' Then he drove along the no. 39 bus route all the way into town. Only on Dublin Bus!

Overheard by Dan

Maybe he was bored?

On a broken down train from Maynooth, stuck somewhere near Connolly station. Darkness. Awkward silence. After a few minutes the driver attempts to reassure the passengers, 'This is the driver speaking ... or is it?'

Overheard by Caoimhe

Busted on the Luas!

On a crowded Luas, coming from the centre of the tram a child's voice says loudly, 'Daddy, why are we on the Luas when we've no tickets?'

Overheard by Yvonne

Indecent proposal

A couple on the no. 79a bus:

Boy: 'Marry me?'

Girl: 'We are on a f**king Dublin bus, you just ruined the most important moment in my life!'

Overheard by Helen @HelenGormley

Stating the obvious

The driver on the bus at Dublin Airport, on the sight of flashing police lights: 'There's something going on, that's all I can say.'

Overheard by Ruaidhri @razorc1

Healthy start to the day

'Without tea and a smoke in the morning I don't think I'd be able to live anymore,' said by a sixteen-year-old on a Dublin bus.

Overheard by Grace @Gracieee_D

Death ride

An elderly woman boarding a rush hour Dart at Pearse Street says, 'Ohh Mary, we're going to be killed ... I know we are!'

Overheard by Shane @Kavo85

Waste not, want not

A woman on the no. 7 bus: 'Thank God the water restrictions are over. My Jimmy will be happy. Poor man, I've been making him pee in the garden all week!'

Overheard by Brian

Oh dear

A taxi driver complaining about 'foreign nationals': 'They don't speak proper English, like what we do and they don't even learn their kids English!'

Overheard by Dexy @DexySmiths

Are they commissioned on dispensing misery?

A Ryanair attendant gleefully asked, 'Can I claim this one?' when a passenger's luggage was too big.

Overheard by Anonymous

At least he got the message

I was on the way home from work on the no. 18 bus. A mother and her child got on in Crumlin. The child proceeds to annoy his mother for money, sweets, etc. After quite a while of this, the mother says to the boy, 'Do you think I shite money, Sean?' Not fazed by this refusal, Sean continues asking for stuff only to be given a response of, 'Ask me hole, Sean.'

Overheard by Carmel

That's gas

'You know what I'm just thinkin'? Where does the Luas stop for petrol??'

Overheard by Gaz @GazCoughlan10

Bono's gaff

Two Dublin lads are trying to impress some female
Spanish students on the no. 46a bus. As the bus
drives past the Mansion House one of lads says,
'That's where Bono lives!'

Overheard by Larry

All the stars

I was chatting with a taxi driver in Tallaght and he
says to me, 'We're getting all the stars over these
days, Neil Young, Robbie Williams and even that
sexy one, Ribena.'

Overheard by Handsome

Two wha'?

On the bus, a young guy says to the bus driver,
'Two please.' The bus driver replies, 'Two what?
Bags of crisps?'

Overheard by Anonymous

Theologians

Two Dubs on the no. 15 bus chatting about Easter:
'Judas got a raw deal, St Peter was just as bad.'

'Ah yeah but Judas was the one who ratted on Jesus!'

Overheard by Abigail

Eye of the tiger

Two drunks on the Dart chat up some Spanish girls:
'Where in Spain are you from?'

Spanish girls: 'Bilbao'

Guy: 'Where?'

His friend: 'Where Rocky's from, ya prick!'

Overheard by Breag

Gotta love the taxi drivers

A Goth girl walks past a taxi rank in Dundrum wearing a full Goth outfit, including blue hair.

Taxi driver: 'Hallowe'en was last week, love!'

Overheard by Sarah @Sarahcasey80

Don't upset the livestock

Aboard an Aer Lingus flight from JFK to Dublin.

Captain: 'We will circle and land shortly; the runway is inundated with rabbits and hares.'

Overheard by Clodagh @ClodaghNee

Best holiday ever

During the Dublin Bus strike: 'Did ye enjoy your few days off?' a passenger asks to the bus driver as he gets on the bus.

Overheard by Ross @RossMullen

You can never be too sure

I was boarding a Turkish Airlines plane at Dublin Airport. A middle-aged Irish woman in front of me asked the Turkish flight attendant, '… tell me now, have ye enough fuel?'

Overheard by Anonymous

An interesting hobby

On the no. 43 bus, a guy says to his friend, 'Why do you always sit at the front?' The friend answers, 'So I can check if the drivers of oncoming buses wave at our driver.'

Overheard by Orla

The hard of hearing pensioner

On a train from Limerick to Dublin, there was the following request over the loudspeaker: 'Would the gentleman who didn't pay for his breakfast please return to the dining carriage?' Everybody looked around and laughed, hoping to see him heading to the dining car. Ten minutes later we heard, 'Would the gentleman who didn't pay for his breakfast, and left his pension book, please return to the dining carriage?'

Overheard by Diarmuid

Not so great expectations

Two girls on the no. 46a bus.

Girl 1: 'I'm looking forward to seeing *Great Expectations*.'

Girl 2: 'What's it about?'

Girl 1: 'Er, it's based on the book.'

Girl 2: 'Oh is there a book?'

Overheard by Ronan

What an achievement!

Two lads on the Nitelink bus.

Lad 1: 'I'm almost twenty-six and I've nothing to show for it!'

Lad 2: 'That's not true, you're nearly bald – not many twenty-five-year-olds can say that!'

Overheard by Anonymous

A bit harsh?

No. 31 bus announcement: 'Smoking is illegal on buses, offenders will be fined.'

Lady: 'Don't fine them, shoot them all.'

Overheard by Myriam @Myriamrive

Fair play

Two girls on the Dart.

Girl 1: 'Sean cheated on me!'

Girl 2: 'Why don't you just leave him?'

Girl 1: 'Cause I've cheated on him so many times that it wouldn't be fair.'

Overheard by Anonymous

One's expendable

On a flight back to Dublin, the overhead bin opens and two bottles fall on a man. A women shouts out, 'Are the bottles okay?'

Overheard by Steve @stevemathers

Anyway ...

In my taxi tonight I overheard a conversation between a young couple in the back of the car.

Young lad says to girlfriend: 'The clocks go forward tonight.'

His girlfriend: 'What do you mean? Clocks only go forward! I've never seen a clock go backward!'

After a few seconds of silence, the young lad says to me, 'So, did you see the hurling match earlier?'

Overheard by Anonymous

Least of her worries

A fifteen-year-old girl on the no. 7 bus: 'I don't know how I'm going to feel about getting married, because I really like my last name.'

Overheard by Anto @AntoMulholland

For the birds

A man on his phone on the no. 123 bus says, 'Can I give you a ring when I get home? I want to keep playing *Flappy Bird*.'

Overheard by Karen @karenchamp

Multicultural

Two gents on the Luas Red Line: 'Ya know Blaine, he got an iPhone 5 off the Travellers and got it unblocked by the Chinese.'

Overheard by Conor @ConorK50

Reassuring

Was on a Ryanair flight and tried to turn off the air from the air vent, when the thing came off in my hand. The flight attendant was passing and took the cap off me with a very comforting, 'Jesus, I swear this plane is falling apart!'

Overheard by Liam

Kids of today

On the no. 37 bus.

Kid 1: 'For my wish, I'd want the power to fly!'

Kid 2: 'I'd use my wish for an iPhone 5.'

Overheard by Gerard @gerrytastic

Cliffhanger

On the no. 39 bus, a man upsets his girlfriend. A random passenger says, 'Could you please sort this out quickly? I have to get off in a few stops.'

Overheard by Anonymous

First class on Ryanair

On a Ryanair flight to Stansted.

Girl: 'Excuse me, flight attendant, can I have a Diet Coke with no ice!?'

Flight attendant: 'Want a little umbrella in there too, princess?'

Overheard by Jenny

Lazarus

Two elderly men meet on the no. 46a bus in Dún Laoghaire: 'Ah Jaysus, Mick, how are ya, I thought you were dead!'

Mick: 'No! I got better!'

Overheard by Katie @Katiemse

Every penny counts

A passenger on the no. 39a bus pays with a load of coppers and the driver says, 'It's a feckin' bus, not a Trócaire box.'

Overheard by Graham @Gralala

Stick with the day job

On the evening of the Rihanna concert, a Ryanair pilot has a bit of fun with his announcement: 'It's very rainy in Dublin this evening folks, so you might want to contact Rihanna and ask her for an umbrella, -ella, -ella.'

Overheard by Emma

Join the dots

Two girls chatting on the Luas Green Line:

Girl 1: 'Did you get off with Sean last night?'

Girl 2: 'It was perfect, do you know what he did? He counted all of my freckles!'

Overheard by Neil

Bus banter

Announcement by the bus driver on the no. 27 bus on Dame Street: 'Please remember to take all your belongings with you when you leave, especially children and old age pensioners – they don't sell so well at auction.'

Overheard by Keith

It's a date!

A geeky guy on the Dart: 'We're definitely going out. I poked her on Facebook!'

Overheard by Anonymous

Anything for a day off

On the no. 49 bus.

'It's a holy day, why are we going back to school today?'

'But you wouldn't go to mass if we were off!'

'That's not the point!'

Overheard by Anto

Fickle fan

On the no. 7 bus.

'What's with the Chelsea schoolbag, don't you support United?'

'I like City now and Liverpool too.'

'Basically you like whoever wins?'

'Yeah.'

Overheard by Jason

Not getting it

Overheard on the no. 46a bus: '... taking our jobs and social welfare money too! If there was a country with no immigrants, I'd move there!'

Overheard by Anonymous

So inconsiderate

Overheard on the no. 78a bus: a lovely girl is complaining that her fella '... robbed a size 12 pair of Levis when he knew I was a size 10!'

Overheard by Jordan

Classy-air

Overheard on a Ryanair flight: 'My co-pilot today is Johnny Murtagh. It's not the jockey, but he does love a good ride.'

Overheard by Joe @_JoeMitch

Smooth operator

While getting on the no. 109 bus from town to Navan, the bus driver turns to a woman of about sixty and says, 'Bejaysus, that's a gorgeous perfume you're wearing. That would encourage a hen to lay, so it would.'

Overheard by Anonymous

Ab-tastic

On the Ballymun bus, two lads are showing off to a group of girls:

Boy 1: 'Look at me sixpack!'

Boy 2: 'That's not a sixpack, they're f**king hunger lumps!'

Overheard by Noel

Little sympathy

Two women are chatting on the Luas:

Woman 1: 'I think he has OCD.'

Woman 2: 'No, he has ADD.'

Woman 1: 'What's the difference?'

Woman 2: 'OCD is an anxiety disorder, ADD means you're a little bollix.'

Overheard by Anonymous

Sydney

A girl at Sydney Parade: 'A return ticket to Sydney Harbour please.'

Cashier: 'Er, I'm not sure this train will take you that far.'

Overheard by Lauren @ladylarlarxx

Doesn't deserve a response

A girl sitting beside her mother on the Luas says,
'Da just texted me asking do we have a preheated
oven.' The mother replies, 'I'm not even answering
him!'

Overheard by Ken @DunneKen

White smoke

A bus driver actually announced the new pope
over the speaker: 'Now hear this ... We have a
new pope!'

Overheard by Emily @EmCally

Foot in mouth disease

Overheard on a Ryanair flight to Paris:

Flight attendant: 'Sir, would you like to sit next to
your mother?'

Unimpressed lady: 'You mean his WIFE!'

Overheard by Shelly

Taxi banter

On the way home in a taxi last night.

Me: 'Iona Road please.'

Taxi driver: 'What? You own a road? How important
are you?!'

Overheard by Paula @paulatierney909

Off ya get!

A bus driver on the no. 13 bus: 'Next stop for the person who's smoking at the back of the bus!'

Overheard by Jack @Jack_O_C

Where else?

Bus stop conversation:

'Where are ya off to with the empty bags?'

'Shopliftin'.'

Overheard by Emily @EmCally

Paranoid

Overheard a couple on the bus having an argument because she had a dream that he was cheating on her.

Overheard by David @davidwatson23

A surreal moment on the Luas

On the Luas Red Line, the driver comes on the intercom and says, 'I'd just like to advise all passengers that Santa Claus is very real.'

Overheard by Molly

The wonder of the double-decker

I was getting on a bus for the city centre at Heuston Station. The bus was full of country folk returning to the big smoke after the weekend. Everyone was squeezing themselves onto the lower deck and ignoring the frustrated driver's instructions to move upstairs. Finally, when we were all like sardines in a tin downstairs and upstairs was still empty, the driver sarcastically announced on the intercom, 'For god's sake, the top deck moves too!'

Overheard by Blanch

O Holy Night

Lads chatting on the Dart:

'Are you going to the Phoenix Park gigs?'

'No way, I was there last year, all "Bethlehem" broke loose!'

Overheard by Aaron

Sinéad vs Miley

Discussion on the Nitelink:

'Who'd win in a fight between Sinéad O'Connor and Miley Cyrus?'

Conclusion: 'Sinéad would bleedin' batter her!'

Overheard by Noel

Two-faced

On the Dart, a girl is talking on the phone: 'Ah congrats, babe, that's great news, I'm so happy!' She then hangs up and redials: 'Liz! Jenny's marrying that bastard!'

Overheard by Ciaran

No fanfare

On a Ryanair flight. Upon landing in Dublin, late after a bumpy approach: 'No f**king trumpets today.'

Overheard by Eimear @eimear_c

It's not like it's a major street or anything ...

On the Luas, two women are trying to decide which station to get off at:

Woman 1: 'Well, Abbey Street is close to Connolly Street, so I'd say we should get off there.'

Woman 2: 'Connolly Street? You mean O'Connell Street?'

Woman 1: 'Ah, sure. I couldn't be expected to know the name of every street in Dublin. When you come up from Cork, it's like going to a different country!'

Overheard by languagenerd

Calm the jets

The driver of the no.16 bus says to a woman who thought he wasn't going to stop and let her on, 'Of course I was. Chill yourself out there, woman.'

Overheard by Paul @playcock

Fiddling

The driver on the no. 49 bus: 'To the two lads upstairs! Consumption of alcohol is prohibited on Dublin Bus … and take your hands out of your trousers!'

Overheard by Yvonne

The invisible man

A guy on the Luas says to his friends, 'I hate when a
girl says to me, "I wish I could find a guy like you".
Eh, hello, I'm a guy ... just like me!'

Overheard by Dylan

Short cut

Dublin bus driver: 'Honestly folks, it's my first day
doing this route and I haven't a clue where I'm going.'

Elderly man: 'I'll show you a short cut, son.'

Overheard by Anonymous

Identity thief

A foreign woman is getting on the no. 27 bus with
some sort of pass. The bus driver says, 'That's a
bleedin' library card!'

Overheard by Niall @niallcully

Don't mention the war

On a Ryanair flight from Berlin, the flight attendant
says to a German lady, 'Would you mind storing your
handbag away for take-off? Thanks very much, it's
just that the cabin manager's a bit of a Hitler.'

Overheard by Paul

He's just not that into you

Overheard on the Luas Red Line. Three girls, aged
about fourteen, are talking about guys they like. One

girl offers this advice to her friend: 'Ah here, don't bother with him! Remember I asked for his number and he told me it was 999?'

Overheard by flyingcabbage

Sticking up for Madonna

A girl is discussing the upcoming Madonna concert with a friend on the Dart: 'How come sixty-three-year-old Bruce Springsteen isn't too old to still perform but fifty-three-year-old Madonna is slated?'

Overheard by Gareth

Different generation

A girl is excitedly telling an elderly man on the no. 27 bus, 'I just saw Rihanna at the Aviva Stadium!'

Elderly man: 'Rihanna?? What kind of sport is that?'

Overheard by Megan

Bunny boiler

Overheard on the Dart:

Woman: 'I always have to check the oven before I preheat it. My five-year-old likes to hide his pet rabbit in there.'

Overheard by Anonymous

UPC box

A man on the Luas says to his friend, 'I was watching that Craig Doyle show the other night and me bleedin' UPC box went, I ask ya!'

Overheard by Daniel

Special effects

A girl on the no. 27 bus: 'I'm going to see *The Lion King* at the Grand Canal Theatre tonight. It's in 3-D!'

Overheard by Lauren

Nana jokes

A girl on the no. 40 bus: 'My Nana asked me what LOL means. I told her "lots of love". Today she texted "best of luck in your exams, you'll do fine LOL".'

Overheard by Anonymous

Pick up a penguin

A girl on the no. 46e bus: 'I saw a penguin on the beach and I was so happy! I ran over to hug it, but it turned out to be a dog.'

Overheard by Niamh @niamh_hiccups

Multipurpose

On a Ryanair flight to London Stansted.

Woman: 'Two euro for a Twix!'

Flight attendant: 'Well, you can also use it to stir your coffee.'

Overheard by Carl

An apple a day

A man on the Luas is drinking Druids cider: 'Me girlfriend asked me to pick these up ... She's makin' apple crumble.'

Overheard by Sinead @SineadGreenan

New immigration test

Taxi driver: 'You don't qualify as a Paddy unless you can use fifty f**ks in one sentence.'

Overheard by Brian @lavbri

Get it right

Overheard on the Luas Red Line:

Man: 'Tom you're looking well, you've lost weight?'

Tom: 'Yep, I've just completed my third marathon today!'

Man: 'They're called Snickers now, Tom!'

Overheard by Dermot

Desperate times – drastic measures

A man and his young son are on the no. 75 bus.

Man: 'You're two.'

Son: 'No, I'm five.'

Man: 'Do ya want me to have to pay for ya? Then shut up, you're two, alright!'

Overheard by Seán @Kn1ghtmare_

Casual Friday

A man on the no. 46a bus: 'I wore a tracksuit for "Casual Friday" last week, but was told it was too casual! One guy wore an Aran cardigan and that was okay?'

Overheard by Michael

The kinder, gentler and friendlier Ryanair

A Ryanair flight attendant announces: 'Anyone buying tea or coffee can expect FREE milk and sugar.'

Overheard by Finbar

Old habits die hard

An old couple are on the bus, holding hands. He gets an elbow reminding him to bless himself at Harrington Street church.

Overheard by Jen @thisisjenc

Twix

An old man says to the girl sitting beside him on the no. 65b bus, 'I had a Twix today; I haven't had one of those in years – an underrated bar that.'

Overheard by Brendan

Drunken Luas talk

I was standing on the Luas coming from Tallaght one morning and two drunks got on at Heuston. There was a girl obviously going to work, all dolled up in makeup and a black dress. One of the drunks looks at her and shouts down to his mate at the other end of the carriage, 'Jaysus, Jimmy, there's a fine lookin' bird in front of me here!' To which Jimmy replies, 'Is she a fine thing?' The other one starts smiling and leering at her and shouts back, 'She looks da spit of your one, Princess Di.' Then Jimmy just shouts back, 'Before or after the crash?'

Overheard by Anonymous

Damned if you do, damned if you don't

On a full no. 77a bus, an older man offers a lady a
seat, but is met with scorn. He says, 'Ah, you'll never
please a woman with a high arse.'

Overheard by Vinnie @cage_playa

Recessionary times

On Dublin Bus: 'I made a cup of tea last night
without a tea bag.'

Overheard by Joanna @butcherjo

Imagine!

On Dublin Bus.

Teen 1: 'Look at yer man, thinking he's cool with his
John Lennon glasses.'

Teen 2: 'Who's John Lennon?'

Overheard by Darren @DarrenByrne

Saying it like it is

A flight attendant on a Ryanair flight from Dublin to
London Stansted: 'If at any time during our flight you
are unhappy with the service, we have six exits ...'

Overheard by Rory

Sophie's choice

I overheard two guys sitting in front of me on the
bus talking. One says to his friend, 'Have you ever
seen the seventeen on a rainy day when it gets full?

It becomes like a Sophie's choice situation when it
pulls up to a stop ... we can only take one.'

Overheard by Anonymous

Booker Prize

Overheard a woman on the Dart: 'I prefer to read
magazines, I don't like reading books, well except
Facebook of course.'

Overheard by Anonymous

Artficial intelligence

On the no. 25 bus at Heuston Station. A country
lad says to the bus driver, '2.35 please.' The driver
points to the coin box. The lad leans over and
shouts into the box, '2.35 please!'

Overheard by Darren

Role reversal

On the no. 27 bus, a cheeky teenager is asking
her mother, 'Ma, how does it feel to have the best
daughter in the world?' The mother replies, 'I don't
know, ask your grandma!'

Overheard by Rose

The cheeky fecker

On the no. 38a bus a man says to his pal, 'She's a
granny type, you know, in her forties.'

Overheard by Flossy @flossybball

Training wings

Boarding a Ryanair plane, I overheard the pilot say to the cabin crew, 'This is my first ever flight as captain!' That's reassuring …

Overheard by Sam

Maths grinds

In Swords, a kid of about fifteen gets on to a bus going to town. He puts the bus fare, mainly made up of one cent and two cent pieces, into the coin box. The bus driver says, 'And how am I supposed to count that?' Without missing a trick, the kid replies, 'One, two, three ...' and walks on.

Overheard by zebedy

Love/Hate spoiler

A woman on the Luas this morning: 'I was gonna watch *Love/Hate* on the RTÉ player later but my husband spoiled it by telling me the cat dies!'

Overheard by Anonymous

It's true!

On the no. 39a bus from Blanchardstown to town:

'Didn't yer man get shot the other day?'

'Ah sure they usually get shot on Saturdays, don't they?'

Overheard by Graham @Gralala

Histrionics

On the bus into town, a young girl asks her friend,
'Is O'Connell Street named after Paul O'Connell?'
The friend replies, 'Not sure.'

Overheard by Karen @KarenmtKelly

1913 again

On the day of the Lockout commemoration. The
driver on the no. 9 bus: 'I'm taking a detour folks,
O'Connell Street is closed due to the "Lockout".'

Woman: 'Who's locked out?'

Overheard by Dermo

Goose on the M50

A taxi driver says to me as I get into his car, 'You'll
never guess what I saw! I was just on the M50 and
there was a Garda trying to catch a goose!'

Overheard by Anonymous

Finger in the air

Mid-flight from London to Dublin. An impatient
Indian passenger in his sixties, with his finger in the
air to attract the attention of the cabin crew, says to
the flight attendant, 'I've been fingering you for the
last five minutes!'

Overheard by James

Memories

On the Nitelink, a guy says to no one in particular,
'Tin openers. Remember them?'

Overheard by Alan @alanbourke

The Wile West

On the no. 27 bus: 'My Ma's going to see *West Side Story* tonight.'

'What's that?'

'I think it's a play, probably about Tallaght or something.'

Overheard by Mick

Food for thought

Overheard on the Luas: '... did you see they've found that god particle yoke, the Hog's Bison?'

Overheard by Siobhan

Bad reception

Overheard on the bus: 'Ah no, sendin' money on the phone? Wha'? Sure, if the reception was bad, you'd lose half of it!'

Overheard by Delorentos @delorentos

Maternal love

Overheard on the bus: 'Scarlet for meself? I'm scarlet for me ma for having me!'

Overheard by Maeve @maeveos

What time is it?

Overheard on the Nitelink:

'Jayo, what time is it?'

'Er ... I think it's sixty-seven per cent.'

'No, that's your phone battery life, ya drunk eejit!'

Overheard by Declan

Random Ramblings

In the blink of an eye

At College Green: 'Gotta pop into Boots 'n' pick up a pack of eyelashes.'

Overheard by Elka @Elka72

Country cousins

In Mountjoy Prison.

Prisoner: 'I don't want to be searched!'

Officer: 'You're being searched!'

Prisoner: 'This is racist!'

Officer: 'Get lost, I've cousins in west Clare blacker than you!'

Overheard by Anonymous

Holiest place

Overheard at the Eucharistic Congress. A seventeen-year-old making his way into 'youth space' at the RDS says, 'This must be the holiest place in Dublin tonight!'

Overheard by Lorna

Priorities

Overheard at the gym: 'Education is important, yeah,
I'll agree with you on that. But, biceps are importanter!'

Overheard by Kari @KariVanHorn

Boozy milkshake

'Can I have a dash of vodka with my milkshake?' asks
a lady in Eddie Rocket's at two in the afternoon.

Overheard by Jack @Jack_O_C

SOS – a 'Piercing' sound

I was queuing in the chipper, *Mamma Mia* was on
TV in the background. A large bald man piped up,
'Jaysus, hearing James Bond sing makes me feel so
better about my life.'

Overheard by Helen

French fries

Guy and girl in McDonald's order food, then wear
the face off each other as they wait. 'Are you having
fries with that?' I asked.

Overheard by Trish @TrishaNugent

Lethal snowboard

I was booking a taxi to the airport last night. This is
how the conversation went:

'Hiya, I just booked a taxi and forgot to say that I
need one that will fit a snowboard please.'

Man on phone: 'And, eh, how big is it?'

Me: 'About six foot, I suppose.'

Man: 'Right so it's more of a decoration piece than a weapon then?'

Me: 'The snowboard?'

Man: 'Oh, a snowboard! Jaysus I thought you said a sword!'

Overheard by Ali

Some things never change

At Dublin Airport.

'So, are you the eldest in your family?'

'Yeah, always have been.'

Overheard by Brian @brianfitz236

Saint Keith

A teenage girl says to her friend in Tesco in Rathfarnham, 'It's great the way Keith Duffy is the patron saint of autism.'

Overheard by Jess @JessDoonan

Out of this world

Larry Gogan's 'Just a Minute Quiz' on radio 2FM.

Larry: 'Where's the Mir Space Station situated?'

Caller: 'Emm ... Germany?'

Larry: 'No! Space!'

Overheard by Peadar

McHug

Two lads in McDonald's in Dublin 12.

'Give us a salad.'

'Ah John Joe, going to McDonald's for a salad? It's like going to a prostitute for a hug!'

Overheard by Anonymous

What?!

At yoga class.

'Let the core magnet of the earth anchor your spirit to the ground as you move to warrior pose.'

Overheard by James @JamesDBrando

Heating the Lord Mayor's house

A couple queuing up to see the moving crib at the Mansion House noticed a woman holding a sign that said 'Mansion House Fuel Funds' and said to each other, 'That's a disgrace, I'm not giving money to heat the Lord Mayor's house! It should be for St Vincent de Paul. Terrible!'

On exiting the crib they asked another 'Fuel Funds' collector, 'Why are you collecting for the Mansion House fuel?' The girl nicely replied, 'Eh, I used to think that too when I was a child, but we're collecting money to buy fuel for the poor!'

Overheard by Maurice

The North-South divide

Talking to a lad from Terenure, I said something about Cabra. He asks, 'What is Cabra? Isn't that a snake?'

Overheard by Rachel @rachelobeirne

The female Jedward

An old lady says to a woman with twin babies, 'Ah they're gorgeous, what are their names?' The woman replies, 'Jennifer and Julia, or, as my husband calls them, "Julifer".'

Overheard by Louise

Great question!

A schoolboy reacts to his mother's commiserations after his GAA team lost: 'How come no one ever says "It's only a game" when their team wins?'

Overheard by Anonymous

Justine?

My father on listening to Justin Timberlake: 'She's a lovely singer.'

Overheard by Sinéad @sineadboolynch

Multi-tool

I watched a kitchen knife demonstration: 'So sharp it could cut through the head of a hammer.' A woman asks, 'Does it cut bread?'

Overheard by Mick @mickmc1

What ya having?

Two customers (one pregnant) queuing in Leo Burdock's chipper.

'What are you having?'

'Cod and chips.'

'No, I mean boy or girl?'

Overheard by Dar

Everyone has limits

At Bloom in the Park. 'I'd never get a garden fountain, it's so pretentious,' said a woman wearing an Armani jacket, a Chanel bag and Gucci sunglasses.

Overheard by Joe

The Chinese way

At Bloom in the Park, a middle-aged woman buying a 'Chinese' plant whispers to the vendor, 'I put this in my husband's food, it's better than Viagra.'

Overheard by Kate

A good friend

Overheard a guy saying to the pharmacist in Boots, 'A friend of mine has herpes and I don't know how to get rid of it.'

Overheard by Angela

Getting into the spirit

On Bloomsday, in a small room within Martello tower.

A man, overwhelmed by the occasion, asks, 'Is here where they actually had breakfast?'

Overheard by Anonymous

Pretend cheese?

In Domino's Pizza.

Cashier: 'We now use real cheese!'

Customer: 'What did you use before?'

Cashier: 'Er, I don't actually know.'

Overheard by Rachel

Social dilemma

A teenage girl in Jervis Centre looks at her smartphone and exclaims, 'My life is over ... my Ma just joined Instagram and she's following me!'

Overheard by Greg

Niceness

Girl 1: 'He could see through your fake niceness.'

Girl 2: 'I wasn't being fake.'

Girl 1: 'Well, your American niceness.'

Overheard by Niamh @niamhsherlock

Nice

'When sent to the shop for "a packet of nice biscuits", don't come home with just a packet of Nice biscuits.'

Overheard by Padraic @redcaff

Story of our lives girls

Two middle-aged women are waitressing at a private function one night, waiting on the last couple to finish their starters in order to begin bringing out the next course.

Waitress 1 says: 'Are they finished yet?'

Waitress 2 says (in all her innocence): 'He's finished, she's not, story of our lives, girls!'

Overheard by Anonymous

Re-dial

'Did you just hang up on me?! I wasn't finished giving out!'

Overheard by @concretecollar

At least she's honest

At Ben Dunne Gym in town.

Trainer: 'So, what's your favourite machine at the gym so far?'

Woman: 'Honestly? The vending machine.'

Overheard by Willy

Kinky boots

TV3 weather report: 'Good evening, well it certainly was fifty shades of grey across the country today!'

Overheard by Andrew @andygarrigan75

Mysterious muffin

At Dublin Airport security point, a guard tells a woman carrying coffee and a muffin, 'You'll have to drink the coffee here and we'll need to scan your muffin.'

Overheard by Christy

Life experience

At the Dublin Horse Show.

'I'm looking for my sister Zoe, she's on work experience.'

'Ah yes, she's out the back relieving one of the stable lads.'

Overheard by Alan

Some women are never happy

'... he kept promising me the moon and it just never happened.'

Overheard by Christopher

Excess baggage

'So Ryanair is taking a case against Channel 4, I hope it's under ten kilos!'

Overheard by Jimbo @jimboireland

Man child

A man, woman and a screaming child are in Dublin Zoo. The woman says to the man, 'For f**ks sake,

Sean, you can't tell a four-year-old to suck it up and walk!'

Overheard by Kevin @kevinegan32

Bus ride from middle earth

On bus back from Slane Castle.

'Harry's going to get sick!'

'Five points to Gryffindor!'

Overheard by Annette @Nettyburns

Puppy love

In Cabra.

'How long are you with your new bird?'

'A month and a half.'

'A month and a half and you already have a puppy, Jaysus!'

Overheard by Warren @ItsWar10

Moose

'Aw, the meal was lovely. It came with a moulin bouche and all.'

'An amuse-bouche?'

'No, there was no moose in it.'

Overheard by Dunny @DunnyMac

What did they expect, a free bottle of whiskey?

At the end of the tour in the Old Jameson Distillery during Culture Night two men are chatting: 'Do you remember when you would get a free can of Coke after the tour at the Coca-Cola factory? So what's the deal here?'

Overheard by Ruth

Generation gap

In St James's Hospital, an older nurse says to a younger nurse, 'I found my old pager. I'm thinking of selling it on eBay, it could be seen as retro.' The younger nurse asks, 'What's a pager?' The older nurse replies, 'It's like a tweet, only twenty years ago.'

Overheard by Paula

Vitamin C – full boost

A man in Boots pharmacy: 'Can I get a packet of Vitamin C, 200 megabytes, please?'

Overheard by Shaun

The unwilling volunteer

In a Dundrum charity shop.

Glam lady: 'Are you still looking for volunteers?'

'Yes.'

'And would they get paid?'

Stunned silence.

Overheard by Keavy @KeavyL

Yeah, that will work

An electronic cigarette salesman in Tesco: 'Smoking is cool again!'

Overheard by David @dnuge

The power of advertising

In Ballybrack Credit Union, looking to get a two thousand euro loan: 'Please, your one Imelda May sent me!'

Overheard by Keith @Mosfido

Back and sides

Overheard at Sam's Barbers: 'Personally I would prefer a number three back and sides, but my girlfriend hates my ears.'

Overheard by Graham

Stick it back in!

Dublin Airport, a US immigration officer says to a teenage boy, 'Please stick your thumb out and put it on the glass scanner. No, not your tongue, sir!'

Overheard by Mick

A metaphor fail

Overheard in RAW Condition Gym.

Personal trainer: 'If you don't buy a ticket, you can't win the raffle, so finish that rep and buy a ticket!'

Woman: 'What raffle?'

Personal trainer: 'Never mind!'

Overheard by Stevie

What direction?

A woman on the Belfast train in Connolly (which can only go north) is asking people, 'Which direction will the train be going?'

Overheard by Aaron @aoneill147

Gotta stay loyal

Overheard in my local bookies: 'I can't bet on any other meeting while Cheltenham is on, sure it would be like cheating on the wife!'

Overheard by Paddy @paddyccourtney

Good excuse!

Overheard a woman in the queue for the toilet at Heuston Station: 'Let me in ahead of you. I've had five kids!'

Overheard by Clara

Time out

A girl in Eddie Rocket's, Blanchardstown: 'I hate it when the hour goes forward. I get all jet-lagged for the whole week!'

Overheard by Rachel

Trying to stay warm

At Bobo's Burgers on Camden Street after the rugby game: 'Jaysus, it was so cold in the pub, I'm having a sexual relationship with this radiator!'

Overheard by @beansybeansy

Hasn't got a clue!

During the Austria vs Ireland game. A guy (hipster type) in The Bernard Shaw keeps shouting, 'Come on, Kilbane!' every time Seamus Coleman is on the ball.

Overheard by Mark

I axe you

Two middle-aged women in a chipper:

'One single, please. I'll get this.'

'You will not. I'm paying for it, you got the Tic Tacs earlier!'

Overheard by Steve @stevebroncolane

Project Maths

In the GPO on O'Connell Street: 'Can I have three dozen stamps please?'

Assistant: 'Sorry, we only sell them in books of twelve.'

Overheard by James @Carlislef1

Escaping the inevitable

Overheard a Dub in Tramore during the heatwave: 'It's just as well she died in May, as this heat would have killed her.'

Overheard by Rory @rorymcevoy

The upset plant

Woman in work: 'When I got home on Friday my plant was so upset . . . I had to pull five orange leaves off it . . . Was very upset.'

Overheard by Angela @Ang_stef

Summer in Dublin

Man on the no. 122 bus has a can of Devils Bit cider in one hand and a Magnum ice cream in the other. It's officially summer in Dublin!

Overheard by Darren @RadioCleary

Drink Aware

In Kehoe's pub, a French guy asks for, 'Three Cokes please!'

The barman, mishearing him, says, 'Three Carlsbergs, great,' and went and put them on.

The French guy says, 'I said three Cokes, not Carlsberg. But Carlsberg will do.'

Barman responds with, 'Good man!'

Overheard by Brian @MrBrianBennett

A biology teacher, no less!

'Why is it that every time I open my mouth to talk, someone starts talking?'

Overheard by Jenna @Steviesluvchild

The Social Life

Suspicious minds

'People are never as suspicious as they are when you are an Irish man in a pub who is not drinking alcohol.'

Overheard by Danny @Dannywilsonirl

Balanced diet

A woman ordering brunch in Odessa restaurant asks the waiter, 'Can I have a double Bloody Mary please?' Then she turns to her friend and says, 'That's two of my five-a-day now!'

Overheard by Shauna

Coffee fix

A businessman walking into 3FE Coffee says, 'Seriously, if they're out of Guatemalan beans, I'm gonna kick a child.'

Overheard by Richie

Desperate

Two old fellas are watching SkyNews in the Halfway House pub.

Old fella 1: 'Did you see that David Beckham is giving his wages to charity?'

Old fella 2: 'Have you ever seen anyone so f**king desperate for a knighthood?'

Overheard by John

He's in trouble now ...

A guard is searching a young lad at Oxegen.

Guard: 'Do ya have anything on ya that ya shouldn't?'

Lad: 'Yes, me da's socks!'

Overheard by Anonymous

Picky, picky!

A small group of women chatting in Bewley's on Grafton Street:

'Are you ever going to get married, Siobhan?

Siobhan: 'Not a chance, I like sleeping diagonally!'

Overheard by Dave

Requests

Two lads are playing guitar in the Temple Bar pub. A drunk guy shouts, 'Here, do you do requests?' One of the lads replies, 'Yes', and the drunk guy says, 'Well f*ck off, cause you're bleeding brutal!'

Overheard by Anonymous

Silent mode

The announcer in the theatre says, 'Please turn off anything that may disturb the performance.' A man at the back quips, 'Me wife!'

Overheard by Claire @delacyx

Cup of coffee

The barista at 3FE Coffee asks a woman, 'Can you sense that pleasing grape acidity with a hint of cherry and apple?' The woman replies, 'It just tastes like Nescafé to me!'

Overheard by David

Wham!

A lad is watching the Rose of Tralee in a Cabra pub: 'Ah yeah, a great personality, but she has a face like a camel chewing a Wham bar.'

Overheard by Tony

What do you take me for?

A man hands his drink to the woman with him while he goes to the toilet. The woman looks at him with disgust and says, 'I don't hold beer!'

Overheard by Nikki @TheWanNonly

Identification fail

A young fella shows his ID in a pub in town. The barman says, 'This doesn't look like you.' He replies, 'It does, he's my brother!'

Overheard by Alison @anmhiabu_

You can take the guy out of Cork ...

After the Dublin vs Cork game, a guy from Cork asks for Guinness in the Brew Dock pub, there is none. A Dublin girl shouts, 'You should be drinking Beamish!'

Overheard by @bluenosenemesis

Ah you're grand

At the Palace Bar, a tipsy English guy says, 'I just want to apologise for eight hundred years of occupation and for that bastard Oliver Cromwell!'

Overheard by Niall

Couldn't give a shite

A girl in the Metro cafe chatting with a friend: 'I like men who are "self-defecating" and who don't take themselves too seriously.'

Overheard by Jack

Piano man

At the Billy Joel concert. After Billy introduces his bass player, a girl asks her exasperated boyfriend, 'Who's on piano?'

Overheard by Karen @munnellk

Touchy-feely

A guy and a girl were on what seemed like a first (and possibly last) date in Crackbird restaurant. The guy said, 'I'm a touchscreen kind of guy.'

Overheard by Mick

Geography grind

Chris Brown at the O2: 'Dublin, you're my favourite city in the UK!'

Overheard by Cormac

Asylum

A girl says to the barman in Grogan's pub, 'Do you have menthol cigarettes?' The barman replies, 'No, we've a lot of mental people, but not cigarettes.'

Overheard by Damian @damianbyrne01

Keeping it in the family

In Butler's café, a woman is gossiping with friends about her ex-husband's new squeeze, 'I call her my wife-in-law.'

Overheard by Anna

A touchy tale

A girl smoking outside the George pub admits to her friend, 'I only play tag rugby so I can feel up other girls.'

Overheard by Olivia

Big brother

A guy at the bar in Fibber Magees pub: 'I couldn't believe what the judge knew about me. He knew more about me than I did!'

Overheard by Phillip @BriBriOnTour

Dress code

In a pub in Tallaght.

Guy 1: 'This weekend I went into town with no jacket, very rare that happens.'

Guy 2: 'What about trousers?'

Overheard by Mark @markjsobrien

Apple soup

In a bar in Dublin 22 at lunchtime, a customer in his thirties asks the barman for a menu. The barman goes to take the order. 'What's the soup?' asks the customer. 'Tomato,' says the barman. 'Ah jaysus, I hate tomato, give us a pint bottle of Bulmers so.' The barman says, quick as a flash, 'Would you like brown or white bread with that?'

Overheard by Phil

Tipping point

At Herbstreet restaurant at the Grand Canal.

Lady to waiter: 'I'll tip you five euro, even though you dropped a fork on me.'

Husband: 'I'd have tipped you fifty quid if that was a knife!'

Overheard by Anonymous

Mafia magic

Outside the Grand Canal Theatre after a showing of *West Side Story*, a girl asks her boyfriend, 'Well, what did you think of that? Didn't I tell you it was good?' The guy replies, 'Ah yeah, it wasn't bad. It was a bit like *The Godfather* but with the gay mafia.'

Overheard by Hannah

Genetic warfare

In Kylemore café, a couple are having a tiff. The woman comes out with this gem: 'Well if we ever do have kids, it'll be your fault if they're ugly.'

Overheard by Tina

On the fiddle ...

In a pub that has traditional music every Thursday: 'Why's there no music this evening?'

Barman: 'No room, sure how could ye fiddle in weather like that?'

Overheard by James @jpflanaga

Gas

'Arthur's Day … immediately followed by Farter's Day.'

Overheard by Conor @conmanwalsh

Bandwagoners

In Copper Face Jacks nightclub, I spotted two young ladies asking every lad in a suit if he was 'on the Clare team'.

Overheard by Darren @darrenor

Blown away

Overheard at a Sigur Rós gig in the O2: 'Thank f**k the tickets were free, I don't even know these, they sound like bleedin' helicopters!'

Overheard by @Mondoburley

Get 'em young

'But I thought it was legal on Arthur's Day!' says a young lad to a Garda while drinking on the street.

Overheard by Alan @apmonaghan

Ask a stupid question

In The Exchequer bar.

Punter: 'What's that?'

Barman: 'It's a handheld wood chip smoker.'

Punter: 'What does it do?'

Barman: 'It smokes!'

Overheard by Enda @Endawaters

Could a child be more disappointed?

In Cornucopia restaurant. 'Oscar, do you want to share a chickpea salad?' a mother says to a profoundly disappointed five-year-old boy.

Overheard by Ben

Thirsty

In the Gresham Hotel after the All Ireland Final, two girls ask for two pints of Carlsberg. The barman says, 'No Carlsberg glasses left.' The girls ask, 'Got any buckets?'

Overheard by Bryan @hicksonb

Suspicious minds

An old man in the Starbucks café, College Green:
'I only asked for a coffee. What do you want me
name for?'

Overheard by Anonymous

Breaking bad

Overheard at the Electric Picnic:

Girl says to friend: 'What's the correct etiquette for
acquiring weed?'

Friend: 'Ummmm, I'm not sure there is an "etiquette".'

So the girl then approaches a random guy: 'Have you
any weed?'

The guy: 'Have you any pills?'

Girl: 'I have Nurofen?'

Overheard by Anonymous

Sav blank!

In The Long Hall pub.

Woman: 'I love you.'

Man: 'Is that you or the wine talking?'

Woman: 'That's me talking to the wine!'

Overheard by The Long Hall Pub @TheLongHallPub

Latin lessons

In the Turk's Head bar.

Polish guy: 'Why do Irish people support Celtic? They're Scottish, aren't they?'

Irish guy: 'Two words buddy, Dias Pora.'

Overheard by Dillon

Cup of tea

An old man sitting in Arnotts café: 'Ah yes, the three best words in the English language are "cup of tea".' (He's not wrong.)

Overheard by Anonymous

FFS!

In Winters Bar in Dundrum: 'Like, you know Ronan O'Gara, like, any idea why they call him ROG?'

Overheard by Padraig @Padraigdc

Five-a-day

A woman ordering for her kids in Eddie Rocket's, 'Can I have fries, onion rings and ... what do yous want for your third vegetable?'

Overheard by Chloe

Reality check

After a Stone Roses concert I picked up a guy in my taxi outside Phoenix Park.

Me: 'Working tonight?'

Passenger: 'Yeah, was stewarding at the Stone Roses gig.'

Me: 'Busy?'

Passenger: 'Was crazy buddy ... it was full of forty-year-old blokes pretending they were twenty.'

Overheard by Tony

Ireland's Call

An Irish Rugby fan in the Porterhouse pub: 'I blame "Ireland's Call" for us losing!'

His friend: 'Yeah, that Italian band butchered it.'

'No, I mean the song in general!'

Overheard by Eoin

Calves

At Oxegen festival last year, we were sitting around drinking our cans and having the craic. Someone mentions one of the lads' unusually large calves. Another lad, who wasn't familiar with this fact, asks to see these beasts. Cue his reaction: 'They're not calves! They're a pair of f**kin' cows!'

Overheard by Paddy

Moral priorities

Overheard in a café: 'You can't have that, you're a vegetarian!'

'I'm not a vegetarian when I'm hungover.'

Overheard by Anonymous

A bird in the hand ...

At The Laurels pub, Clondalkin, a customer orders
'Two Bulmers and a Wild Turkey'. The barmaid
looks puzzled. Then she says, 'Sorry we've no
turkey, but I can get you a chicken sandwich.'

Overheard by Anonymous

Busted!

Overheard in Starbucks, Rathmines: 'I think that guy
is eavesdropping on us.'

Overheard by Anonymous

Pub banter

A middle-aged man in Grogan's pub: 'I met a woman
yesterday who said I only look half me age.'

Fellow drinker: 'She must think you're ninety-two.'

Overheard by Pat

Doesn't discriminate

A man is looking at a menu in a fancy restaurant
and says, 'How the f**k do they know it's a Wicklow
wood pigeon?'

Overheard by Niamh @Niamh_Noonan

The bottom line

'Did you hear that "Arthur's Day"-related incidents
were down by fifty per cent this year?'

'Yeah, but I bet you bog roll sales were up one hundred per cent!'

Overheard by Anonymous

SAS

In Molloy's pub in Tallaght, a man who clearly knows nothing about football tries to impress his mates: 'That Suarridge guy is having a good season.'

Overheard by Ciaran

Split personality

At Starbucks café.

Cashier: 'What's your name?'

Customer: 'Dan.'

Cashier: 'But yesterday you said it was Rob?'

Customer: 'So why are you asking me again?!'

Overheard by Gavin

Bad romance

Overheard a twenty-something-year-old girl at the Bruce Springsteen concert in the RDS: 'Bruce Springsteen is, like, twenty years older than my Dad and I'd still marry him, is that wrong?'

Overheard by Robbie

To the point

A Munster vs Leinster game is on TV in Kielys of Donnybrook. A man walks in and asks a woman,

'Any tries scored yet?' The woman replies, 'Er, no, not yet, just conversions.'

Overheard by Anonymous

Scrubs up well

At O'Neill's Bar, a girl tells her friends, 'Oz was so different to Ireland.'

Girl 2: 'Like how?'

Girl 1: 'Well for one, you have to shower every day.'

Overheard by Darren @darrenor

Working in Starbucks ... literally

A woman on a laptop in Starbucks complains to the barista, 'The CD you're playing is on loop!' The barista replies, 'Maybe you should work from a real office, then?'

Overheard by Anonymous

You Casanova!

A man says to a woman on a dinner date in Milano, 'You have eyes like a cow, in a good way!'

Overheard by Jade

Lost in translation

In O'Neill's pub, an Irish girl stands up and says, 'I'm going out to smoke a fag,' to which her American pal replies, 'You're gonna shoot a gay guy?!'

Overheard by Anonymous

Have we bottled it?

A young lad on the no. 27 bus: 'Gonna get me fake ID later for Arthur's Day. Can't wait man, gonna get smashed!'

Overheard by Neil

Born free

A customer at Crackbird, the chicken restaurant: 'Is your chicken freelance?'

Overheard by Richard

Third time's a charm?

Overheard in Starbucks café, Ballsbridge: 'Ah you've obviously got some likable qualities, you've been engaged twice.'

Overheard by Evelyn @EVIEALKIN

Tayto head

Overheard in a pub in Tallaght:

Customer: 'Can I have a packet of Tayto?'

Barman: 'Is King okay?'

Customer: 'Is monopoly money okay?'

Overheard by Chris

High as a bike

Overheard in Grogan's pub: 'You have to admire anyone winning the Tour de France on drugs. When I'm on drugs, I can't even find my bike!'

Overheard by Dean

The Sublimely Silly

Weight watchers

Two women are chatting after a weight loss group meeting:

Woman 1: 'I don't like that instructor!'

Woman 2: 'Why?'

Woman 1: 'I prefer the one we had last week, she weighs you lighter!'

Overheard by Oisin

What's good for the gander

Larry Gogan's 'Just a Minute Quiz' is on radio 2FM. Larry asks, 'What was Gandhi's first name?' The caller answers, 'Eh ... Goosey Goosey?'

Overheard by Anonymous

Now that we'd love to see!

At Dún Laoghaire library, a man asks the librarian, 'Do you have any books with photographs of dinosaurs?'

Overheard by Ruth

Security threat?

At Dublin Airport.

A security officer asks a man, 'Any liquids or gels in your bag?'

Man: 'No, just me sangwiches.'

Overheard by Aoife @flanners28

First time bet

A girl pulls out her betting slip and says, 'I've got 2.30 to 1 on this!' Her companion replies, 'No love, that's the time the game starts.'

Overheard by Mark @MarkMolloy9

A bag please

A woman in a Chinese takeaway: 'I'll have a spice bag without the spice.'

Overheard by Snanne @1suzannie

High altitude

On the summit of Howth Head, a group of girls are enjoying the warm weather. One says, 'I need a cigarette, the air is awful thin up here!'

Overheard by Claire

Staying alive

Overheard a girl in the IFSC talking about her Mum's goldfish, 'It is ten years old, ten years old, and it has never died.'

Overheard by Aine @aineekennedy

Checking in

Overheard at Dublin Airport security control: 'No, of course you don't put your baby in the tray, you can carry him through with you!'

Overheard by Catriona

Rip-off

At the Gaiety School of Acting, a group of students are discussing *The Hobbit*. A girls says, 'It's the biggest rip-off of *Lord of The Rings* I have ever seen!'

Overheard by Allana

He's a sharp one

A girl outside the Grand Canal Theatre says to her boyfriend, 'Look! *Cats* the musical is coming to Dublin!' The boyfriend laughs, 'Cats can't sing!'

Overheard by Abbie

Repressed veggie?

Two girls are talking about the creation of the 'stem cell burger'. One girl says, 'I don't want to eat a burger from a dead cow!'

Overheard by Iano

Value for money

I was waiting to be served at the customer service desk in the local Dunnes Stores.

Assistant 1: 'There's a woman on the phone, said she checked her receipt when she got home because it seemed a bit high, she says she was charged for three bottles of wine but she only bought two. What'll she do?'

Assistant 2: 'Tell her to bring back the receipt.'

Assistant 1 (after a short pause): 'Now she wants to know, does she bring back the bottle?'

Overheard by Anonymous

Astronomy argument

A couple are having an argument outside the Baggot Inn. She says to him, 'The earth doesn't revolve around you, Gavin, you're not the moon!'

Overheard by Joe

Nelson who?

In the Dublin Wax Museum: 'You don't know who Nelson Mandela is? He's only the most famous African American ever!'

Overheard by Colm

And the Oscar goes to ... miaow

Overheard a young girl talking about the new *Love/ Hate* episode: 'How'd they get the cat to play dead anyway?'

Overheard by Sean @seankeogh27

The root of the problem

'Urgh! Why are these vegetables so dirty?' Overheard at the organic farmers market in Temple Bar.

Overheard by Ethan

It's addictive stuff

Overheard on Baggot Street: 'D'ya ever get an adrenaline rush from Facebook likes?'

Overheard by Evelyn @EVIEALKIN

A weapon?

At Dublin airport.

'Do you have anything that could be mistaken for a weapon?'

'Well, just me hair straighteners.'

Overheard by Linn @wittster

Sharon

In a Ben Dunne Gym, SkyNews is on TV. The headline reads, 'Sharon dies after eight years in coma.'

Two women seem shocked: 'Is that Sharon from *X Factor*?'

Overheard by Ardan

Chips

In a chipper, a young girl asks for some chips. The man behind the counter says in an Italian accent, holding up one finger, 'One chip?' The girl replies, 'One chip? No, lots of chips!'

Overheard by Líam @McLiamo

Are you shaw?

In the lift in Mercer Street car park. A guy asks his girlfriend, 'Are we far from The Bernard Shaw?' The girl replies, 'Who? Doesn't he make ham?'

Overheard by Mary @MaryMc_31

Ask a silly question

At a wedding in Clontarf Castle, a guy asks the waitress how the beef is done. 'In the oven,' she answers.

Overheard by John @Jonner2102

The stupid leading the blind

In Dundrum Town Centre, I overheard a woman tell a blind man 'over there'.

Overheard by Anonymous

Imagine that!

A lad in Dublin Zoo reaches in and touches a sheep in the petting farm. He turns and says to his friend, 'Jaysus, that feels like wool!'

Overheard by Roy @tricky7373

Not so near

'And where are you from?'

'The Philippines.'

'Oh right ... is that near Palmerstown?'

Overheard by Jordie @Jordie_Fordie

Falling H₂O

Overheard in Ballsbridge: 'Wet rain is the worst kind!'

Overheard by Evelyn @EVIEALKIN

Fields of gold

A group of women are on a train home to Dublin:
'We need the rain, the grass isn't even green, that's
terrible.' They were looking at barley.

Overheard by Ewan @EwanMacKenna

Good question

I am driving along with my thirteen-year-old
daughter and her two friends in the back seat. They
are talking about endangered animal species and my
daughter says she read about an endangered bird
that only breeds every five years. 'How does it hold
its breath for that long?' asked one of her friends.

Overheard by John

Pump it up!

At the Esso petrol station on Strand Road, a man says
to the woman at the adjacent pump, 'Prices have
gone crazy.' The woman replies, 'I don't care how
much they raise the price, I only get twenty euro
every time.'

Overheard by George

Italian birds

I was on the Dart out to Howth this morning and
two tracksuited young men were sitting near me

talking about the recent mysterious mass bird deaths in Arkansas:

Fella 1: 'Wha' type o' birds were they?'

Fella 2: 'I dunno, crows or blackbirds or sometin'.'

Fella 1: 'And the same thing happened in Italy yesterday!'

Fella 2: 'Yeah. I saw dah on Yahoo.'

Fella 1: 'Bu' they were doves or sometin' over there.'

Fella 2: 'Ah yeah, de Italians are much more sofistica'ed!'

Overheard by Muller

Who'd be a security officer?

Overheard at Dublin Airport security control:

'Remove your shoes please.'

Man: 'Both of them?'

Overheard by Anonymous

Pretend heat

In a smoking area: 'It's really warm out here, even if it's artificial heat.'

Overheard by Aidan @sweeney_aidan

The Olympic spirit

A girl in Dundrum Town Centre: 'The Winter Olympics are boring, there's nobody famous in it. *Dancing on Ice* is much better!'

Overheard by @Anorack_Jack

Kilometre girl

A girl at the five mile run in Phoenix Park: 'I've never run miles before ... only kilometres.'

Overheard by Declan @decollery

Wasn't that, Newton?

'He's goin' to be the next Steve Jobs.'

'Who de hell is that?'

'Yer man who invented the apple.'

Overheard by Gillian @gillianroseduff

The secret's out

In Milano restaurant, a girl says to her friend, 'It's, like, SO unfair that Victoria's Secret is only in the airport, Victoria Beckham should open more!'

Overheard by John @CooleyGBA

Worlds apart

A girl meets her friends in town: 'I need a coffee, I'm so jet-lagged!'

Friend: 'Where were ya?'

Girl: 'I spent the weekend in Paris.'

Overheard by Gareth

Turn the other ...

'They named the child Paige?'

'Yeah, sure, they're always reading books.'

Overheard by Peter @PJDublin8

The real world

At Dublin Central Library, a man asks: 'Do you have a globe?'

Librarian: 'We have a table-top model.'

Man: 'Don't you have a life-size model?'

Librarian (pauses): 'Yes, but it's in use right now.'

Overheard by Sean

Spice girl

Overheard a girl ordering a chicken wrap in Azteca Deli:

Girl: 'Is your salsa chicken very spicy?'

Deli assistant: 'Not really, it's very mild.'

Girl: 'Ah great, I don't like spicy food.'

Deli assistant: 'Anything else?'

Girl: 'Yes, can I have hot chilli sauce and some jalapeños?'

Overheard by Frank

The Wisdom of Young and Old

Alive and Kicking

A woman beside me in a coffee shop asks, 'How old d'ya think I am?'

Me: 'Seventy?'

Woman: 'I'm eighty-four next week.'

Me: 'Wow! What's your secret?'

Woman: 'Vegas!'

Overheard by Irish Gal @Moules11

Mind the family jewels

In a Marlay Park playground, a little boy says to a little girl as they are playing on a seesaw, 'Stop going fast, you're hurting my boy parts!'

Overheard by Stephanie

Baby blues

Two old women are chatting in the ILAC centre: 'Poor Mary, she's suffering terribly with the post-mortal depression.'

Overheard by Paul @Ryanofoto

Busted

Overheard in a public toilet in Blanchardstown: 'But Mammy, Daddy always lets me not wash my hands!'

Overheard by Shane @Kav_Kavanagh

Move the dial

Two elderly ladies on the no. 29a bus:

'I'll miss Pat Kenny in the mornings.'

'But he'll be on Newstalk.'

'I don't have Newstalk, Bernie!'

Overheard by Eileen

Technology isn't what it used to be

At a phone shop in Crumlin, an elderly man is asking about different phones, colours, etc. Just as the young sales guy was about to take the order for a Nokia, the man says, 'Does it have a toothbrush?' The sales guy looks all confused and checks with other staff to see if there is an offer of some kind on. The elderly man says, 'Sorry, son, I meant Bluetooth.'

Overheard by Skeg

Casual Friday

A three-year-old boy is at Easter mass. During a moment of silence, he asks in a loud voice, 'Nana, why is the priest wearing his dressing gown?'

Overheard by Killian

Awww ...

Two lovely old ladies on a bus: 'I don't have a mobile, I like the surprise when you answer the phone and can't see who's ringing.'

Overheard by Naomi @NaomiD12

What about Pac-Man instead?

A nine-year-old boy is in the Temple Street Hospital day ward.

Nurse: 'Do you want to play Xbox?'

Boy: 'Yes, can I play *Grand Theft Auto* please?'

Overheard by Barry @Pogo_1972

Misinterpreted

Two old ladies on the no. 150 bus discuss the end of Trapattoni's reign as the Ireland football manager: 'I feel sorry for his daughter.'

'Ah yes, a lovely girl, always by his side helping him with the English.'

Overheard by Grainne

You can't fault her logic

Mother: 'We're having cheese sandwiches for lunch.'

Girl: 'I don't like cheese.'

Mother: 'You do like cheese.'

Girl: 'I don't.'

Mother: 'You like cheese on pizza.'

Girl: 'That's not cheese, that's pizza!'

Mother (exasperated): It's the same ... oh well, what do you want in your sandwich then?'

Girl: 'Pizza.'

Overheard by Anonymous

Rose-tinted view

A small boy is walking with his daddy in St Stephen's Green.

'Dad, what colour is Tuesday in your head?'

Dad: 'Hmmm?'

Boy: 'It's purple for me. Wednesday is yellow, Thursday is ...'

Overheard by Declan

What a coincidence!

On the no. 51b bus on the way to the city centre, two old ladies behind me are having a quiet ramble.

Lady 1: 'My husband died when he was eighty-two.'

Lady 2: 'That's the number of my door! The other way around!'

Overheard by Aine

What a show

After a very long sermon at mass, a little boy of about two, clapped his hands and yelled out, 'Yeah, all done now!'

Overheard by Joe

Vertigo

Two old women are talking about a pair of high heels: 'Jaysus, you'd get a feckin' nose bleed in them they're so high!'

Overheard by Courtney @CourtneyBoyce_

Once upon a time

At mass in Bray, a little boy says his prayers loudly: 'God, will you look after Mammy, Daddy and all the people eaten by the angry giant in giant-land.'

Overheard by Diarmaid

What next!

A car crashes into a bus and an old lady, who is being transferred to a new bus, says, 'A murder in Dublin yesterday, now this.'

Overheard by Roy @tricky7373

Global perspective

Overheard a young boy on a Ryanair flight to London Stansted: 'Daddy, are we outside of the earth right now?'

Overheard by Katelyn

Sarcasm isn't wasted on the old

My Nanny, my Mam and I were walking out of SuperValu when my Nanny spots a fella that she knows walking towards us really slowly with a walking stick. She says to him, 'Jaysus, Michael, out runnin' marathons again, are ye?'

Overheard by Anonymous

Sense of scene

A child on a tour of the Old Library in Trinity College says, 'Ma, this looks like a room from Hogwarts in *Harry Potter*!'

Overheard by Oscar @CynicalOscar

Wrong direction

In Argos, Santry. An older woman asks, 'Have you got the half-cast One Direction fella in stock?'

Overheard by Andrew @mcgowaner

Teach 'em young!

A youngish mammy and her five-year-old daughter get stuck in a pedestrian bottleneck in Penneys, O'Connell Street. The mammy says, 'What do you say when people get in your way?' The daughter goes, 'Gerrout of me f**king way!'

Overheard by Pete

Knitting

At the no. 49 bus stop at The Square in Tallaght: 'If the young ones of today just put their mind to it, they could do knittin'!'

Overheard by Jo @KeyesJo

Naughty but nice

In Dunnes Stores on Grafton Street a little boy, about five years old, is walking around the lingerie section shouting, 'Knickers, knickers, knickers!'

Overheard by @unrulyupstart

When you sprinkle ...

At The Oval Bar.

Two old men finish up at a urinal:

'Jaysus, if I shook mine that much, it'd fall off!'

'Ah, sure, it's the only shakin' I get these days!'

Overheard by Ronan

Wildlife

I was at Dublin Zoo last year with my girlfriend and we were walking behind a family. One of the kids exclaims, 'Look Daddy, a bee!' The dad looks bemused, turns to his daughter and says, 'We come all the way to the zoo and you're amazed by a bee!' He should have saved money and gone to the park instead.

Overheard by Bren

The sense of it all

At Eason's in Liffey Valley Shopping Centre. A little boy asks his dad, 'Why do the books in this library have prices on them?'

Overheard by Lisa @TheMagentaBook

Why bother?

An elderly man in the newsagent's this morning: 'So many dying lately. It's a terror to be alive at all.'

Overheard by James @Carlislef1

For life, not just for Christmas

I was in work one day in Liffey Valley, and just before I completed the customer's purchase I offered him one of our long-life bags.

Me: 'Would you like to buy a "bag for life" today, sir?'

Customer: 'What would I need another bag for life for, I've got one standing beside me!' He pointed to his wife, and she dug him in the ribs quite hard.

Overheard by Lulu

Marco!

In IKEA, an Italian lady is excitedly calling her husband to look at some curtains: 'Marco!' A little girl nearby: 'Polo!'

Lady: 'Marco!'

Girl: 'Polo!'

This went on for a bit.

Overheard by Anne

Old wisdom

A granny says to her granddaughter, 'iPad? You know what I had to play with when I was your age? "Outside", that was it, now you try it.'

Overheard by Avril @FoleyAvri

Trying to sneak a kiss

I was walking back home from school in the afternoon. A little boy, about nine years old, starts going along beside me on a scooter.

Little boy: 'Can I have a kiss?'

Me: 'Nope, you're too young for me.'

Little boy: 'I am 16, I swear … I am just a midget!'

Overheard by Aisling

Sshhh

On Dublin bus: 'Ma, will ya tell him to shut up, I wanna tell God something!'

Overheard by Sarah @psychpoigirl

Auld ones united

Working on a busy ward in St James's Hospital, I went to see an elderly demented lady who was in a bay of four beds with three other ladies. All four had been there a few days and during the course of their admission they had become very pally and caused all sorts of problems such as comparing who had the best commode, best nurses, best doctor etc.

As part of a general orientation check, I asked the lady if she knew what day it was. She took a few moments and eyed up her fellow patients and said, 'Well, between the four of us, we've decided it's Tuesday.'

Overheard by Anonymous

Contraception Dublin style

I was on the no. 123 bus into town. Beside me, there is a mother with two screaming kids and, I assume, their grandfather. Getting off the bus the old man says in a strong Dublin accent, 'I'm not having any more grandchildren, I'm going on the pill.'

Overheard by Daniel

Moral advice

In a doctor's waiting room in Cabra.

An old man says to a young lad: 'Are ye married?'

Young lad: 'No.'

Old man: 'Good man. My advice, son: get yourself a maid.'

Overheard by James

Sex education Irish style

In Jo'Burger, a little boy asks his auntie, 'What does "lesbian" mean?' The auntie explains, 'It means that I love girls.' The little boy says, 'Oh! I'm also a lesbian. I love girls, too!'

Overheard by Mick

Client server

Overheard a man in PC World, Jervis Centre: 'In my day, "client server" was another name for shop assistant.'

Overheard by Niall

A little bit racist?

My granny was talking about flying ants: 'They're like Spanish students – loads of them all over the place in summer!'

Overheard by Pilates Plus Dublin @pilatesplusdub

A Freudian slip?

My Nana said to my cousin the other day, 'Oh did you enjoy your First Erection concert?'

Overheard by Niamh @neeerv

Opportunity spotter

A little boy in Smyths Toys tells his Dad, 'Mammy said she wants a Captain America Transforming Dart Shield for Mother's Day!'

Overheard by Grainne

Sounds sore

An old man comments on a group of Goths, 'Look at them dressed up like that. Sure I suppose they're only young and the haemorrhoids are at them.'

Overheard by Anonymous

Good luck!

In Tallaght, a young boy scout with a cut knee leaves the doctor's clinic.

Doctor: 'Good luck with being a boy scout!'

Boy scout in all sincerity: 'Thanks, good luck with being a doctor!'

Overheard by Sophie

Holy chips

I was in Silvio's chipper in Rathfarnham, queuing behind a woman with a young child. When they got their chips, the man behind the counter asked the usual, 'salt and vinegar?' The woman replied 'yes' so he added both. The child, on seeing the man putting on the vinegar, says, 'Mammy, why is that man baptising my chips?'

Overheard by usher

Thanks for asking

An old man says to a woman, 'You've lovely teeth, are they your own?'

Overheard by Paul @PaulMcQuillan76

Free Willy

A man in Dublin Zoo says to his child, 'Now what's that?'

Child: 'An elephant.'

Man: 'What do elephants have?'

Child: 'A big willy.'

Man: 'No, that's his trunk, pet.'

Overheard by Aisling @AshhMaher

A bank teller's nightmare

An old fella is applying to open a bank account at Bank of Ireland in Coolock:

Cashier: 'Do you have a passport, sir?'

Old fella: 'No, never had one of those!'

Cashier: 'Okay, do you have a driver's licence?'

Old fella: 'No, sure I've never driven a car in my life.'

Cashier: 'Could you supply us with a telephone bill?'

Old fella: 'No, I've never had a telephone in my life.'

Cashier: 'Sir, do you have any identification to prove who you are?'

Old fella: 'Sure what do I need identification for? I know who I am!'

Overheard by Anonymous

Feeding time at Dublin Zoo

A young girl watching the sea lions getting fed at Dublin Zoo says to her mother, 'Do you not think it's about time we got fed, Mam?!'

Overheard by Emily @EmCally

Pope update

An old man is walking up Dame Street, when he momentarily stops at a bus stop with a large queue of people and proclaims, 'We're still popeless!' and walks on.

Overheard by Killian

Accountants get a bad name

I'm an accountant. I went to a client's house in Santry to get his tax return signed. His young lad (about four years old) answers the door and runs back into the hall shouting, 'Da, Da, it's the f**king tax man!'

Overheard by Colin

Green man

An old man, not willing to wait for the green man at a pedestrian crossing in Finglas: 'Ah, the little green bastard must be on a lunch break!'

Overheard by Anonymous

Birth day

In terminal 2 at Dublin Airport.

Little boy: 'Mammy what date am I born on?'

Mother: 'On 1 July.'

Little boy: 'That's the same day as my birthday!'

Overheard by Stephen @_stemcgrane

You young lads!

Old woman: 'Does this bus go to O'Connell Street?'

Me: 'Nah, it doesn't.'

Old woman: 'I don't believe you young lads!'

Overheard by Ross @RossMullen

Ramadan a ding dong

Irish kid: 'Is your uncle over on holidays for Ramadan?'

Indian kid: 'No.'

Irish kid: 'That's the only time of year you eat, isn't it?'

Overheard by Richie @richie_no_t

A feisty sister

I was in Blanchardstown Shopping Centre, sitting down on a bench. A woman and her two kids were sitting beside me. The young lad (about ten years old) was messing, doing karate kicks at his younger sister and he accidentally kicked her in the stomach. Instead of the usual tears you'd expect, she just shouted at him, 'You kicked me ovaries!' and then went to kick him between the legs.

Overheard by Anonymous

Perspective

Overheard two pensioners in the post office: 'You know the old story, we're only a germ on earth.'

Overheard by Paul @PaulMcQuillan76

Hashtag

A little girl is getting ashes for Ash Wednesday and asks, 'Teacher, are we getting a hashtag?'

Overheard by Ruth @ruthells1

He was close enough

Pensioner in Dunnes Stores, Tallaght: 'I'm going to grill my chicken for dinner on my new "George Formby".'

Overheard by Rob @TeggyRob

An interesting metaphor

A little girl is lying on the grass in St Stephen's Green Park, gazing at the sky and she says, 'Mammy, the sun is a girl and the clouds are boys.'

Overheard by Anonymous

Word on the Street

Scouser

Man 1: 'I hear they're trying to find a recording of Jim Larkin's voice for the Dublin Lockout Centenary. Apparently his accent was Dublin with a bit of Scouse.'

Man 2: 'He probably sounded like Ronnie Whelan!'

Overheard by Gary

Stay away from that house

'He's strange, strikes me as one of those people who hands out fruit at Hallowe'en!'

Overheard by Avril @FoleyAvril

The injustice of it all

'Now they want to ban smoking in cars? What's next? Banning smoking while you're pregnant?'

Overheard by Adrian

New Irish

Two stallholders on Moore Street, one African, the other Chinese, are having some banter:

African man: 'Your tomatoes are banjaxed!'

Chinese man: 'Ah go on out of that!'

Overheard by Tony

Deconstructing stereotypes

An elderly Dublin man at the St Patrick's Day parade laughs at a group of Americans holding a banner, 'I've been Irish for eighty-two years and I've never said "Top o' the morning" to anyone, ever!'

Overheard by Andrea

Alms giving

A man outside Centra on Dame Street asks a woman, 'Do you have three euro for milk and bread?' The woman replies, 'Sure, I'll buy it for you myself!' He hesitates, 'Could you get us two cans of cider instead?'

Overheard by Rebecca

Practice what you preach

A man says to an Amnesty chugger, 'Isn't it ironic how Amnesty International opposes the "persecution" of people when they are experts in it?!'

Overheard by Ross

Text politics

On Grafton Street, a girl is complaining to her boyfriend, 'Why didn't you reply to my text?' The boyfriend answers, 'How am I meant to reply to LOL?'

Overheard by Ciara

Jack sprat

Overheard from a flat window in Gardiner Street:
'Hey! Assummmptah! Come in here if ya want the
skin off yer father's rasher!'

Overheard by Anonymous

Dalkey dilemma

A girl on Aungier Street is talking on her phone:
'Go out to Dalkey? I'd rather get sick on myself!'

Overheard by Ben @Ben_Brogan

Disorientation

Overhead a phone conversation at Gay Pride,
Merrion Square:

'I'm on the west side of the square, beside the beer
tent … that's the south side, are ye sure? Well, my
orientation's never been great.'

Overheard by TexasEx

Surely there are laws against that?

I just overheard somebody say, 'My boss is trying to
pigeon me hole.'

Overheard by Anonymous

Going for gold

Overheard on Dawson Street, at the Ireland Olympic
Team homecoming: 'Jaysus, if "shouting" was an
Olympic sport, Michael Ring would get gold, the
fecking eejit!'

Overheard by Anonymous

The writings on the wall

Writing on a wall near the Four Courts: 'Free Palestine' and written underneath, 'F**k that, Free Dental! Lisa needs braces …'

Overheard by Donal

Fifty shades of green

A friend was standing at a traffic light, eyeing up a guy she fancied. An old man in a car behind her shouts, 'Is it a particular shade of green you're waiting for?'

Overheard by Monica @Monbling

Chancer

A Viking Splash Tour bus drives by: '... and to the left here we have Trinity College, where the infamous Book of Spells is kept!'

Overheard by Stephen

Actually a good idea

A man in the queue outside Kilmainham Gaol says, 'You'd think they'd employ someone to sing rebel songs to the people waiting in line.'

Overheard by Savage Henry @carldogs

The price is right

My Ma on a drive over to the south side: 'Oh look, there's Ailesbury Road, that's real expensive on the Monopoly board!'

Overheard by Jen @jenhatton

Sliding scale

One of a group of young-looking lads says to the bouncers outside the lap dancing club Lapello, 'So, on a scale of one to ten, how much am I not allowed in?'

Overheard by Eva

Nature nurture

Overheard in Rathmines during very stormy weather: 'This wind is great! It's giving my hair loads of volume!'

Overheard by Orla

Straight to the point

Two lads are walking past George's Street Arcade and one of them says, 'So yeah, anyway, long story short, she drove a car through the front door.'

Overheard by Conor @Genocide_Juice

Animal activist

A man's reply to a PAWS chugger outside Bruxelles pub: 'Sorry love, I don't believe in animals.'

Overheard by Richard @rfrankdoyle

Celtic codology

As the Aircoach passes by Croke Park, a Spaniard, appearing all knowledgeable about Dublin, turns to his newcomer friend and says, 'That's where Celtic play!'

Overheard by Derek

Terrible loss

A man walking down O'Connell Street says, 'Ah feck it! I hate it when I lose a sneeze!'

Overheard by Declan

Invasion of privacy

An Amnesty chugger on Dame Street cheerfully says, 'Hello in there!' to a woman wearing a burka.

Overheard by Daire

For emergencies only

At the IFSC, a businessman on his mobile phone was walking by and said, 'Ryanair?! No, I'm not flying Ryanair, that's just for emergencies.'

Overheard by Eoin

Winging it

A driver on the Viking Splash Tour says, 'That used to be Jonathan Swift's house, has anyone heard of him?' A young girl hazards a guess, 'Taylor Swift's Da?'

Overheard by Ruth @RuthKerins

Self-assessment

On Leaving Certificate results night: 'He's not that drunk, he can still remember his CAO number!'

Overheard by Shane @hogey143

Should come with a health warning

Folks on the Viking Splash Tour at College Green scream, 'Aaaarrrrgghhhhh!!!!' A startled old man says, 'F**k off ya gobshites! I have a pacemaker!'

Overheard by Richie

Tourettes

A young fella of about fifteen is on a date with a girl. I can sense the awkwardness and then he comes out with, 'What's it like to wear makeup?'

Overheard by Jade @jade08kinsella

What a coincidence!

Overheard in the queue at Xtra-vision for *Grand Theft Auto*'s midnight release: 'Hey, are you here for *Grand Theft Auto*?'

Overheard by Anonymous

Phoenix Park tour

Walking past the Wellington monument, a country lad says to another, 'What's that, Sean?' Sean replies, 'Eh, Nelson's knee or some shite.'

Overheard by Conor @ConorK50

Nothing but the best

A girl in Herbert Park says to a woman walking her dog, 'Your dog's coat is to die for! The woman replies, 'I know. It's a Philip Treacy.'

Overheard by Caitlin

Rainbow robbery

Two women admire a rainbow over Dublin bay:

Woman: 'Isn't it beautiful, Mary?'

Mary: 'It is, but I preferred rainbows before the homosexuals hijacked them.'

Overheard by Anonymous

Window cleaner

A mother says to her son outside Tesco in Phibsborough, 'No licking the windows!'

Overheard by Neil @noriordan

Scale of tracksuit to chino

A guy on the phone is talking about areas to rent: 'Well if you consider the ratio of tracksuits to chinos, it's practically downtown LA!'

Overheard by Mimi @aunt_mimis

Blame it on the weatherman

'I don't mind the rain, it's the forecaster's lies I can't stand.'

Overheard by Shanners @RandomSaint

Happy ending

A teen discussing *Love/Hate*:'I was sent out of the room 'cause Nidge was in a brothel. Me Ma never called me back in, so I don't know how it ended.'

Overheard by @Fairport_Fee

That's more than half!

A girl on phone says, 'I'm not saying every fella from Kinsealy is bet down, but a good seventy-five per cent are.'

Overheard by Zoe @shesamaniac86

A blonde moment

In Parnell Park, a lad says about his mate, 'He got his hair done ... he's now a peroxide ginger!'

Overheard by Noel @noelk16

Recovery required

A woman (finally) leaving the new National Driver Licence Service centre: 'That was worse than getting my gallbladder out!'

Overheard by Anonymous

Money can't buy class ...

'No such thing as bad weather. It's bad clothing on people!' says a woman wearing a dead fox over her shoulders.

Overheard by Therese

Worst excuse ever

A man on his mobile phone: 'Listen, I have a case of nose whistle syndrome. I think I'll have to cancel the theatre.'

Overheard by Gillian

Brand loyalty

Written on a placard outside Marks & Spencer in Mary Street: 'Not just any strike, this is a Marks & Spencer strike!'

Overheard by Brenda @crinklecutchips

Sheep

I was waiting at the bus stop when a young kid steps up and says, 'Here we are ...' and as everyone stands up, the young kid sits down and says '... waiting on a bus.'

Overheard by Keith @Mosfido

Twit

A man at Dublin City's New Year's party: 'My resolution for 2014 is to be less social and more social media! So I'm going home to tweet!'

Overheard by Holly

Flood warning

Two elderly men are discussing the flooding around Ireland: 'Where's Enda Kenny, why isn't he sandbagging?'

Overheard by Anonymous

In the doghouse

A kid crawls into a kennel outside a pet shop. His mam says, 'Ah would ya get out of there? It's your da who's in the doghouse!'

Overheard by Ann Marie @PartAnnMarie

Plead the fifth

'I'm saying nothin' and I'll keep on saying it.'

Overheard by Joseph @PhilMelia

It's all relative

'Are you from Kerry?'

'Am I f**k, we have shoes, I'm from Midleton!'

Overheard by David @DavidLeBas0

Bunch of bankers

'You bastards!' a girl is shouting outside Bank of Ireland as they lock the door in her face at 3.59 p.m.

Overheard by Thomas @NightLord2009

So very true

'If it wasn't for the culchies, Garth Brooks would only be playing one gig in the Olympia.'

Overheard by @ Anorack_Jack

So close and yet so far

Woman: 'I'm going to see *Fiddler on the Roof* tonight.'

Man: 'Ah nice, I love Tennessee Williams!'

Woman: 'You're thinking of *Cat on a Hot Tin Roof.*'

Man: 'Whatever, I was close.'

Overheard by Luke

Generation clash

At Spar in Dame Street. The Clash song 'Rock the Casbah' is playing on the radio. A teenage girl in the queue is singing along, 'lock the taskbar, lock the taskbar ...'

Overheard by Deirdre

It's no sacrfice

'One week off chocolate today!'

'Fair play to you, Siobhan, that must be difficult?'

'Oh it is, but the white chocolate is a great substitute.'

Overheard by Eimear

Wonders of the world

'I didn't know the Eiffel Tower was man-made!'

'I know! And the Spire as well!'

Overheard by @Ariannebooklove

Shatter that illusion?

Overheard at the St Patrick's Day Parade: 'Good to see the Garda band being led by a whistleblower!'

Overheard by Patrick @PatrickBury

Daylight robbery

'I'll tell ya where they can stick their property tax. At least Dick Turpin wore a mask.'

Overheard by Gavin

Singing the blues

I was out walking my two dogs.

A lady: 'What are their names?'

Me: 'Jazz and Bassie.'

Lady: 'Aghh, the auld blues music!'

Overheard by Andrew @andygarrigan75

Wish me luck as you wave me goodbye

Two guys meet outside the Social Welfare Office on Bishop Street:

Guy 1: 'Hey! What are you doing here? I thought you were on one of those JobBridge schemes?'

Guy 2: 'The bastards let me go after two months!'

Guy 1: 'No way! Did you get a reference at least?'

Guy 2: 'No, but I did get a sorry-you're-leaving card and a f**king One Direction Easter egg!'

Overheard by Tony

Logical son

A teenage boy is walking up O'Connell Street talking on his mobile: 'Yeah Ma, I know money doesn't grow on trees! That's why I'm asking you for it!'

Overheard by Kevin

We've all been there

Two friends bump into each other in town.

'How's the new job?'

'I'm going home to spend the rest of the day in the foetal position.'

Overheard by Ray

Money only

A chugger on Westmoreland Street: 'Do you have a minute?'

Man: 'Yes, I have a minute but I have no money, love.'

Charity worker: 'Okay, have a nice day!'

Man: 'Er … but I said I have a minute.'

Overheard by Ger

Trained

Some Gardaí on horseback pass by two guys.

Guy 1: 'They're trained not to shit on the street you know.'

Guy 2: 'The Gardaí? ... Ah okay, I get ya now!'

Overheard by Emily

Amnesty International

Girl says to an Amnesty chugger on Dame Street, 'I thought Amnesty International was an airport!'

Overheard by Anonymous

Ooops

I passed by two angry female Clare supporters on Henry Street: 'I can't believe he drove to Dublin and left the tickets at home!'

Overheard by Richard @richiemolloy

Is she for real?

On Moore Street.

'Hey Mary, congrats, I heard your Sandra had a baby girl. What's she calling it?'

'Hazel.'

'Hazel? She named it after a nut?'

Overheard by Anonymous

Love/Hate goes south side

Outside BTs on Grafton Street.

Woman 1: 'OMG, is that yer one from *Love/Hate*?'

Woman 2: 'Eh, what the f**k is she doing on the south side?'

Overheard by Shanners @RandomSaint

Shakespeare

A poet recites his work on Grafton Street. A man applauds, 'That's worthy of the Great Bard!' The man's wife says, 'No, it's much better than that, I'd say it's worthy of Shakespeare!'

Overheard by Barry

Nerd play

Dating advice on Dame Street: 'Ya can't wear your Tardis hoodie man, she'll think ya are a f**kin REtardis.'

Overheard by @feminist_fatale

Good question!

'Is it wrong to drop litter on the spot where there used to be a bin before the visit of Obama and the Queen?'

Overheard by Aaron @aoneill147